Media Law in the United Arab Emirates

Media Law in the United Arab Emirates

Second Edition

Matt J. Duffy

This book was originally published as a monograph in the International Encyclopaedia of Laws/Media Law.

Founding Editor: Roger Blanpain
General Editor: Frank Hendrickx
Volume Editors: Peggy Valcke &Eva Lievens

Wolters Kluwer

Published by:
Kluwer Law International B.V.
PO Box 316
2400 AH Alphen aan den Rijn
The Netherlands
E-mail: international-sales@wolterskluwer.com
Website: lrus.wolterskluwer.com

Sold and distributed in North, Central and South America by:
Wolters Kluwer Legal & Regulatory U.S.
7201 McKinney Circle
Frederick, MD 21704
United States of America
Email: customer.service@wolterskluwer.com

Sold and distributed in all other countries by:
Air Business Subscriptions
Rockwood House
Haywards Heath
West Sussex
RH16 3DH
United Kingdom
Email: international-customerservice@wolterskluwer.com

Printed on acid-free paper

ISBN 978-94-035-0020-1

e-Book: ISBN 978-94-035-0021-8
web-PDF: ISBN 978-94-035-0022-5

Printed in the United Kingdom.

The Author

Matt J. Duffy serves as an Assistant Professor at the Communication and Media School at Kennesaw State University in Georgia, USA, where he teaches International Media Law and Journalism. His work has been published in the Berkeley Journal of Islamic and Middle Eastern Law, the Journal of Middle East Media, Middle East Media Educator, and the Journal of Mass Media Ethics. He also serves on the board of directors for the Arab-United States Association for Communication Educators (AUSACE), an organization that aims to improve journalism education in the Middle East. Duffy taught journalism at Zayed University in Abu Dhabi, UAE, from 2010 to 2012.

The Author

Table of Contents

Table of Contents

Table of Contents

List of Abbreviations

ADMIC	Abu Dhabi Media Investment Corporation
AED	United Arab Emirates Dirhams
ANHRI	Arabic Network for Human Rights Information
FNC	Federal National Council
FCC	Federal Communications Commission
GCC	Gulf Cooperation Council
HRW	Human Rights Watch
IAM	Internet Access Management
ICCPR	International Covenant on Civil and Political Rights
ISP	Internet Service Provider
MCYCD	Ministry of Culture, Youth and Community Development
MZA	Media Zone Authority
NMC	National Media Council
U.K.	United Kingdom
U.S.	United States
VoIP	Voice over Internet Protocol
WAM	Emirates News Agency

List of Abbreviations

Acknowledgements

I'd like to thank my former colleagues at Zayed University's College of Communication and Media Sciences in Abu Dhabi, United Arab Emirates, for the opportunity to teach Journalism and International Media Law in the country. Raza Rizvi, a lawyer with Simmons & Simmons, provided invaluable insight into many sections of this book and also provided some of the primary sources. Finally, I'd like to thank Dr. Kyu Ho Youm, the former president of the Association for Education in Journalism and Mass Communication and John Marshall First Amendment chair at the School of Journalism and Communication at the University of Oregon, for suggesting that I write this book.

Acknowledgements

General Introduction

§1. General Background of the Country

I. Political and Legal System of the Country

A. Introduction

1. The United Arab Emirates (UAE) is a federal state formed in 1971 as a union of six Emirates ruled by sheikhs. The six Emirates—Abu Dhabi, Dubai, Sharjah, Ajman, Umm al-Qaiwain, and Fujairah—were joined by a seventh, Ra's al-Khaimah, in 1972. The ruling sheikhs agreed to the federation at the behest of the Abu Dhabi ruler, Sheikh Zayed bin Nahyan, and the ruler of Dubai, Sheikh Rashid bin Said Al Maktoum, as the British forces formally ended its roughly two centuries of protection treaties with the Trucial States, sheikdoms on the eastern side of the Arabian Peninsula. The nearby Arabian Peninsula countries of Bahrain and Qatar had originally planned to join the UAE but they chose to form independent nations when agreements between them could not be reached.[1]

2. Since its formation, the ruler of Abu Dhabi has served as the country's president with the ruler of Dubai or his crown prince serving as vice-president and prime minister. The country has seen only two presidents—Sheikh Zayed and his son, Sheikh Khalifa bin Zayed.[2] The rulers of the emirates are monarchs who have not been elected in popular elections but rather with succession generally handed down through generations.[3] The Federal National Council (FNC), a parliament of forty— members (half elected, half appointed), has the ability to review, comment on, and revise laws but holds no authority to enact or overrule legislation. Article 180 of the Penal Code bans the formation of political parties, and efforts at civil society are discouraged.[4] The government does not allow the formation of trade unions, syndicates, or independent

1. Eric Hooglund & Toth, Anthony, *A Country Study: United Arab Emirates* (Washington, D.C.: Library of Congress, 2007), http://lcweb2.loc.gov/frd/cs/aetoc.html.
2. Christopher M. Davidson, *Abu Dhabi: Oil and Beyond* (Columbia University Press, 2009). In Arabic parlance, "bin" means "son of."
3. Hooglund and Toth, Anthony, *A Country Study: United Arab Emirates.*
4. *Ibid.*

journalists' unions.[5] Each emirate retains a certain amount of autonomy and adherence to federal laws varies from emirate to emirate.[6]

B. Federal State Structure

3. Adopted in 1971, the federal constitution sets up a monarchy with the president serving as the supreme ruler of the country. The original constitution—drafted with help of British advisers[7]—was slated to expire in five years and be replaced with a formal constitution.[8] However, the document was periodically renewed in its original form and then permanently ensconced in 1996 with approval of the Supreme Council of Rulers—the sheiks of the seven Emirates—and an endorsement from the FNC, the forty-member advisory body.[9] The constitution grants overall authority to the president. The vice-president, the cabinet (a council of the leaders of the federal ministries appointed by the president), and a federal judiciary system also receive demarcated powers. The constitution states that sharia, Islamic religious law, is the foundation of the legal system.

4. The Federal Supreme Council (made of up the rulers of the seven Emirates) has ultimate authority over law-writing and executive powers.[10] The Supreme Council ratifies decrees from the president and other laws.[11] Some executive powers are overseen by the Cabinet, the heads of the federal ministries, historically chaired by the Prime Minister, the ruler of Dubai. Some laws specifically refer to review or approval from the Cabinet.

C. Division of Competences Between the Federal and Emirate Levels

5. The government is set up to balance federal control with the desire for individual emirate autonomy. So, for instance, Article 13 of the Constitution allows for federal health care and education. But, Article 23 provides for individual control of oil wealth and economic development in each emirate.[12] The latter provision has created a disparity between the emirates since the largest emirate, Abu Dhabi, holds most of the oil reserves.

6. The UAE's legal system is not uniform, a reflection of the balance between federalization and autonomy required to facilitate the agreements between the disparate emirates. The federal courts oversee all the emirates except Dubai and Ra's al-Khaimah, which have local and appellate courts for each emirate. In each emirate, the country uses a dual system of secular courts for most civil law matters and Sharia law courts

5. *UAE: Media Sustainability Index* (London: IREX, 2009), http://www.irex.org/system/files/MENAMSI09_UAE.pdf.
6. Hooglund and Toth, Anthony, *A Country Study: United Arab Emirates.*
7. Davidson, *Abu Dhabi.*
8. Hooglund and Toth, Anthony, *A Country Study: United Arab Emirates.*
9. *Ibid.*
10. "Political System," UAE interact, accessed January 26, 2016. http://www.uaeinteract.com/government/political_system.asp.
11. Hooglund and Toth, Anthony, *A Country Study: United Arab Emirates.*
12. Davidson, *Abu Dhabi*, 61–62.

for criminal and family law cases. The Sharia courts (administered by each emirate) follow Islamic law but are ultimately overseen by the secular Supreme Court.[13] The lower courts are the courts of first instance and each emirate has a Federal Appeals Court. The Court of Cassation, also known as the Federal Supreme Court, is the highest court in the country and is headquartered in Abu Dhabi.[14] The highest court holds five judges each appointed by the seven-member Supreme Council of Rulers. The Court of Cassation is empowered to decide disagreements between the federal government and the emirates or between individual emirates. The emirates of Dubai and Ra's al-Khaimah do not refer cases to the Court of Cassation.[15]

7. According to the Constitution, all decisions by the highest court are binding and cannot be overturned by the president. However, in practice many decisions are subject to presidential review. Also, many of the country's judges are expatriates who ultimately serve at the discretion of the government. For these reasons, most observers do not consider the judiciary to be truly independent.[16]

8. Each of the seven emirates has its own government which functions independently from (but often in close coordination with) the federal government. The most populous, largest and richest emirate is Abu Dhabi, which consequently has the most robust governmental system. Chaired by the crown prince of Abu Dhabi, the Executive Council is the central governing body, made up of leaders of various Abu Dhabi agencies.[17] In Abu Dhabi and the other emirates, municipalities with local departments are in charge of each of the cities or regions.[18]

D. Special Note on Legal System of UAE

9. The UAE follows a civil law system that is inspired by the Roman and French models as well as Egyptian civil codes of law.[19] There are restrictions on the reporting of court decisions so rulings are not widely available. This lack of transparency leads some observers to say that trends in the application of the law can be hard to spot.[20] Unlike common law countries, the law does not evolve through judicial precedent.[21] According to one defamation lawyer, judicial rulings in the UAE tend to be short and, "don't say very much in terms of judicial analysis."[22] Therefore, the starting point (and often ending point) for any discussion of legality regarding the media rests with the primary legislation. One legal observer noted as well that "new laws in the UAE are

13. Hooglund and Toth, Anthony, *A Country Study: United Arab Emirates.*
14. Dubai also features a Court of Cassation, the highest court in the emirate.
15. Hooglund and Toth, Anthony, *A Country Study: United Arab Emirates.*
16. *Ibid.*
17. "Executive Council - Abu Dhabi," *The General Secretariat of the Executive Council*, accessed May 7, 2013, http://gsec.abudhabi.ae/Sites/GSEC/Navigation/EN/ExecutiveCouncil/picture-gallery.html.
18. Hooglund and Toth, Anthony, *A Country Study: United Arab Emirates.*
19. Faizal Latheef, *Legal System and Practice in the United Arab Emirates* (Dubai, UAE: Habib al Mulla & Company, 2011), http://www.habibalmulla.com/Mediaresource/45041b47-a820-44a8-8f6f-ebdc47c42d91.pdf.
20. Alastair Mullis, *Carter-Ruck on Libel and Slander*, 6th Revised edition (Lexis Nexis UK, 2010).
21. *Ibid.*
22. Raza Rizvi, Personal communication, email, March 31, 2013.

not subject to public consultation and are often enacted with limited if any notice."[23] The descriptions in this book are accurate as of March 2016 but are subject to rapid change.

Furthermore, many observers point out that the judicial system doesn't offer an independent check on the rest of the government, a complaint seen in other Gulf countries.[24] One similarity in these countries is the nationality of the judges. Many of these Arabic-speaking judges are expatriates from nearby countries such as Sudan, Egypt, and Jordan. The judges enjoy a relatively wealthy lifestyle and no guarantees of employment in their home countries. One Emirati commentator (who speaks with relative freedom because his uncle is the Ruler of Sharjah), notes that "many judges are themselves not citizens of these Gulf States, nor are appointments assured for life."[25] The judges, therefore, have little motivation to challenge prosecution, especially with those that deal with sensitive topics, such as criticism of the government.

In 2014, a United Nations inspector concluded that the judicial system was "under the de facto control of the executive branch of the government."[26] The special rapporteur on the independence of judges and lawyers said she was concerned that the state security services had undue influence on prosecutors and judges. The UN expert also reported that state security officers had "'almost systematically' violated due process and fair-trial guarantees that existed under national and international law."[27] The UAE justice ministry responded by pointing out that the country's constitution guarantees the independence of judges and country was committed to the protection of human rights.[28]

II. Geography and Population

10. The UAE is a small country of approximately 83,600-square kilometers, roughly the size of Portugal.[29] The country sits on the Arabian Peninsula bordered by Oman to the north and east and Saudi Arabia to the south and west. The Arabian Gulf lies to the north with Iran on the other side. The emirate of Abu Dhabi is by far the largest of the Emirates with an area of 67,350 square kilometers. The UAE and Saudi Arabia disagree over a swathe of land that the Saudis claim between Qatar and the UAE. The disagreement flared up in 2010 leading to shots fired by naval forces.[30] Maps on some UAE government websites show the country's border touching Qatar

23. Mullis, *Carter-Ruck on Libel and Slander*, 1.
24. Al Qassemi, "Institutionalising the Arab Gulf Governments," para. 7;.Doherty, "U.N. Expert Says UAE Judicial System Controlled by Executive," para. 1.
25. Al Qassemi, "Institutionalising the Arab Gulf Governments," para. 7.
26. Doherty, "*U.N. Expert Says UAE Judicial System Controlled by Executive*," para. 1.
27. *Ibid.*, 7.
28. Doherty, "*U.N. Expert Says UAE Judicial System Controlled by Executive*."
29. "United Arab Emirates," *Central Intelligence Agency: The World Factbook*, November 13, 2012, https://www.cia.gov/library/publications/the-world-factbook/geos/ae.html.
30. Richard Spencer, "*Naval Battle Between UAE and Saudi Arabia Raises Fears for Gulf Security*," *The Telegraph*, March 26, 2010, sec. worldnews, http://www.telegraph.co.uk/news/worldnews/middleeast/unitedarabemirates/7521219/Naval-battle-between-UAE-and-Saudi-Arabia-raises-fears-for-Gulf-security.html.

directly, without any interceding Saudi land.[31] Oman and the UAE reached an agreement in 2003 over the eastern boundaries, although the exact details were not released.[32] Maps show Oman stretching to the south and east with small enclaves inside the UAE territory. Also, the tip of the Arabian Peninsula—the south side of the Strait of Hormuz leading into the Arabian Gulf—belongs to Oman, although it is not connected contiguously to the rest of the country. The vast majority of the UAE is desert with less than 1% of its land mass considered arable. However, the country—particularly Abu Dhabi—sits on vast reserves of oil and natural gas.

11. The population of the UAE is approximately 9.5 million but only about 11% are Emirati citizens.[33] The remaining roughly 8.5 million residents are made up of expatriates, with a majority (4.5 million) coming from the Southern Asia countries India, Pakistan, and Bangladesh.[34] Other expatriates come from other Gulf Cooperation Council (GCC) countries—Bahrain, Kuwait, Oman, Qatar, and Saudi Arabia—other Arab countries, the Philippines, China, and the United Kingdom (U.K.). Many of the lower-paid expatriates are male workers who remit payback to their families in their home countries. Among expatriates, men outnumber women at a rate of 4 to 1. The emirate of Abu Dhabi has the largest population of nationals at around 400,000, followed by Dubai with 160,000.[35]

12. The UAE's Constitution established Arabic as the official language. However, many languages including Persian (Farsi), Urdu, Tagalog, Bengali, Chinese, and Hindi are spoken, with English serving as the standard universal language. The UAE government uses both Arabic and English in its communication and the majority of local media employ one of those two languages.[36]

III. Social and Cultural Values

13. The UAE does not have one single cultural identity or socio-economic status. The country is generally conservative because of the Muslim religion that dominates much of the culture. Residents through the Emirates can usually hear the Muslim call to prayer five times a day, broadcast from ubiquitous mosque minarets. Most Emiratis are Sunni Muslim, and many of the expatriates from other Arab countries or South Asia (Pakistan and Bangladesh and to a lesser extent India) also bring their Muslim traditions. These cultural values place a high reverence on prayer and piety as well as conservative perspectives on women's dress and limitations on their role in

31. "About UAE," accessed January 25, 2013, http://www.cemc.ae/subindex.aspx?Id=169&Lid=1.
32. "United Arab Emirates."
33. http://www.bq-magazine.com/economy/socioeconomics/2015/04/uae-population-by-nationality.
34. Staff, "Expats Make up over 88% of UAE Population," *Emirates 24/7*, April 17, 2011, http://www.emirates247.com/news/expats-make-up-over-88-of-uae-population-2011-04-17-1.381853.
35. http://www.bq-magazine.com/economy/socioeconomics/2015/04/uae-population-by-nationality.
36. Hooglund and Toth, Anthony, *A Country Study: United Arab Emirates.*

society.[37] However, the UAE is considered by some to be the most liberal nation in the Gulf, with "other cultures and beliefs generally tolerated, especially in Dubai."[38]

14. However, the large number of expatriates from Western countries as well as an increased emphasis on attracting tourists creates areas in the country (e.g., shopping malls, theme parks) that appear strikingly similar to a European capital rather than a Muslim country. The local press often reports on this 'cultural divide' that flares up with nationals demanding more done to enforce a dress code of modesty in public places.[39] The government regulates the media with an eye on maintaining its conservative culture—for instance, all websites dedicated to pornography, online dating, or gambling are blocked by order of the federal Telecommunications Regulatory Agency.[40]

15. "National identity" is a matter of growing concern as Emiratis cope with retaining their culture and values amid a globalized local landscape and communication system.[41] The Ministry of Culture, Youth and Community Development (MCYCD) is tasked with retaining the nation's culture through various programs such as performances and festivals. The ministry also encourages young people to enter creative fields such as literature and other media storytelling. The MCYCD formed after the Ministry of Information and Culture was abolished in 2006.[42] Much of the media regulation duties of the defunct Ministry of Information and Culture moved into a newly created NMC, the media regulation agency in the UAE. In 2012, an FNC committee issued a report suggesting a revision in media policy (including the regulations of advertisements and satellite channels) because of the media's effect on the nation's youth and national identity.[43]

---

37. Most Emirati women wear abayas, a full-length cloak, and many local families aren't comfortable with women working or attending school in mixed-gender environments.
38. "United Arab Emirates Profile," *BBC*, November 14, 2012, sec. Middle East, para. 12, http://www.bbc.co.uk/news/world-middle-east-14703998.
39. Chiranjib Sengupta, "*Decoding the Cultural Divide in the UAE*," *Gulf News*, June 2, 2012, http://gulfnews.com/news/gulf/uae/society/decoding-the-cultural-divide-in-the-uae-1.1030647.
40. "United Arab Emirates: OpenNet Initiative," 2009, http://opennet.net/research/profiles/uae.
41. Andy Sambridge, "*Action Plan Call to Secure UAE's National Identity*," *Arabian Business*, August 11, 2011, http://www.arabianbusiness.com/action-plan-call-secure-uae-s-national-identity-415890.html.
42. . "About the Ministry," *United Arab Emirates Ministry of Culture, Youth and Community Development*, accessed January 25, 2013, http://www.mcycd.ae/sites/mcycdvar/en-us/pages/AboutTheMinistry.aspx.
43. "FNC Discusses Policy of National Media Council on Updating Media Laws," June 5, 2012, http://www.uaeinteract.com/docs/FNC_discusses_policy_of_the_National_Media_Council_on_updating_media_laws/49781.htm.

§2. The Media Landscape

I. Overview of Media Markets and Main Actors

A. *Introduction*

16. The UAE is a major regional media producer along with Egypt and Lebanon. Several major pan-Arab broadcasters are headquartered in the UAE including MBC and Orbit Showtime Network. The UAE hosts 14% of the free-to-air channels in the Arab world.[44]

17. Dubai, Abu Dhabi, Ra's al-Khaimah, and Fujairah have set up free media zones to attract foreign investment into the media industry.[45] The media zones (particularly in Abu Dhabi and Dubai) have attracted international news outlets including CNN, Reuters, the Wall Street Journal, and Al Arabiya, although the media zones officially operate under the purview of the UAE's Media Laws. They operate with relative freedom although some reports indicate government officials have tried to sway international journalists through subtle threats.[46] Interviews with journalists at Al Arabiya found that they tend to self-censor if the subject matter could be offensive to their Saudi owners or allies, including the UAE.[47] In 2014, a CNN journalist interviewed an Emirati who spoke about the lack of freedom of speech in his country. Within days the Emirati had disappeared and a few weeks later the journalist, the bureau chief for Abu Dhabi, had been transferred to another location.[48] The local press has not covered the interview or subsequent disappearance.[49]

18. Arabic-language Sky News Arabia—a joint project in Abu Dhabi's free zone TwoFour54 owned by the British BSkyB group and the Abu Dhabi Media Investment Corporation (ADMIC)—launched in 2012. A member of the Abu Dhabi ruling family, Sheikh Mansour bin Zayed Al Nahyan, owns ADMIC.

19. International news is widely available through uncensored satellite TV and the Internet.[50]

20. The NMC, the country's media regulatory body, operates the government's official news agency. The Emirates News Agency (known by its Arabic initials WAM)

44. *Arab Media Outlook 2011–2015* (Dubai, UAE: Dubai Press Club, 2012), http://www.arabmediaforum.ae/en/amo.aspx.
45. Anita Siassios, *Regulation of Digital Content in the UAE—Part One* (Al Tamimi & Co. Law Firm, June 2012), http://www.tamimi.com/en/publication/publications/section-3/june/regulation-of-digital-content-in-the-uae-part-one.html.
46. Roy Greenslade, "*UAE Aims to Stifle Press Freedom,*" *The Guardian*, April 16, 2009, http://www.guardian.co.uk/media/greenslade/2009/apr/16/dubai-press-freedom.
47. Mohammed El-Nawawy & Catherine Strong, "*Job Satisfaction and Editorial Freedom at Al-Arabiya: Balance While Covering Volatile Middle East News,*" *Arab Media & Society* no. 16 (Fall 2012), http://www.arabmediasociety.com/?article=796.
48. http://www.cnn.com/profiles/sara-sidner-profile.
49. Duffy, "UAE Twitter Activist Not Guilty but Still in Custody - Al-Monitor." http://www.al-monitor.com/pulse/originals/2014/07/uae-twitter-imprisoned-not-guilty-activist-cyber-crime.html#.
50. Freedom House, *Freedom of the Press: United Arab Emirates.*

offers wire reports in both Arabic and English. Many local news outlets copy and paste the reports into their publications with or without attribution to WAM.

B. Broadcasting

21. The Emirates of Abu Dhabi, Dubai, Ajman, and Sharjah each own broadcast television stations that are available locally and nationwide (via cable).[51] One report notes the state-owned broadcast channels "provide only the official view on local issues."[52] Some other government-owned stations, such as Dubai One, enjoy a regional audience. Table 1 lists major television stations headquartered in the UAE, most of which are owned by the government. Fully 95% of households in the UAE have a television.[53]

Table 1. Major Television Stations in the UAE

Station	Location	Language	Ownership
Abu Dhabi TV	Abu Dhabi	Arabic	Public, Abu Dhabi Media (Government of Abu Dhabi)
Ajman TV	Ajman	Arabic	Public, Ajman government
City 7 TV	Dubai	English	Private, Mohidin Bin Hendi
Dubai One	Dubai	English	Public, Dubai Media Inc. (Government of Dubai)
Dubai TV	Dubai	Arabic	Public, Dubai Media Inc. (Government of Dubai)
MBC 4	Dubai	English w/subtiles	Private, Saudi Arabia, Waleed bin Ibrahim bin Ibrahim
Sharjah TV	Sharjah	Arabic	Public, Sharjah government

Sources: BBC Media Profiles, Wikipedia, individual websites, accurate as of February 2016.

C. Radio

22. The UAE features more than twenty major radio stations that broadcast in a variety of languages, a reflection of the country's diverse inhabitants. Stations

51. *United Arab Emirates - Media*, United Arab Emirates Profile (London: BBC, June 15, 2012), http://www.bbc.co.uk/news/world-middle-east-14704229.
52. Freedom House, *Freedom of the Press: United Arab Emirates*, para. 6.
53. *Arab Media Outlook 2011–2015*.

broadcast programming in Arabic, Urdu, English, Hindi, Persian, Russian, Filipino, Tamil, and Malayalam.[54]

23. The large government-owned firms Abu Dhabi Media, Dubai Media Incorporated, and Arab Radio Network (a subsidiary of government-owned Dubai Holdings) own most of the radio stations in the UAE. Abu Dhabi Media operates Quran al Kareem (religious programming), a classical music station, Abu Dhabi FM (talk/classic Arabic hits), Classic FM (Arabic and English music), Star FM (Arabic and English Top 40), and Al Emarat FM (Arabic/Emirati hits). Dubai Media Incorporated owns Dubai FM Radio 93 (Arabic music) and Noor FM Dubai (Arabic classic hits). Arabian Radio Network operates Dubai 92 (English adult contemporary), Radio Shoma (Persian music), Hit 96.7 (Malayalam hits), Al Arabiya (Arabic contemporary), Al Khaleeji (music of Gulf countries), City FM (Hindi contemporary hits), Dubai Eye (English news, talk and sport), and Virgin Radio (English Top 40). Few stations are privately owned.[55]

D. Print Media

24. The literacy rate in the UAE is 78% and daily newspaper readership hovers above 50%.[56] The local media features more than a dozen English and Arabic newspapers, all of which are government-owned or government aligned, in part because of the heavily regulated atmosphere.[57] *See* Table 2 for a list of newspapers, their language, and ownership.

Table 2. Major Newspapers/Online Outlets in the United Arab Emirates

Newspaper	Location	Language	Ownership
Seven Days (free tabloid)	Dubai	English	Private, Daily Mail General Trust (U.K.)
Al Bayan	Dubai	Arabic	Dubai Media Inc. (Government of Dubai)
Al Roya (business news)	Dubai	Arabic	Private, IMedia
Al Ittihad	Abu Dhabi	Arabic	Abu Dhabi Media (Government of Abu Dhabi)
Al Khaleej	Sharjah	Arabic	Private, Dar Al Khaleej
Emarat Al Youm	Dubai	Arabic	Dubai Media Inc. (Government of Dubai)

54. https://en.wikipedia.org/wiki/Radio_and_television_channels_of_Dubai.
55. "Radio and Television Channels of Dubai," *Wikipedia, the Free Encyclopedia*, January 14, 2013, https://en.wikipedia.org/wiki/Radio_and_television_channels_of_Dubai.
56. *Arab Media Outlook 2011–2015*.
57. William A. Rugh, *Arab Mass Media: Newspapers, Radio, and Television in Arab Politics* (Praeger, 2004).

Gulf News	Dubai	English	Private, Galadari Brothers Group
Gulf Today	Sharjah	English	Private, Al Nisr Publishing
Khaleej Times	Dubai	English	Private-Public, Galadari Brothers Group and 30% Government of Dubai
The National	Abu Dhabi	English	Public, Owned by Abu Dhabi government

25. The government-owned Al Ittihad, an Arabic-language newspaper based in Abu Dhabi, has served as an official organ of the government since its launch in 1969. The newspaper features pictures of the country's rulers in meetings and other photo opportunities with public officials. The newspaper (like many others in the UAE) often publishes the government news agency press releases without modification.

26. In 2008, the Abu Dhabi government created an English-language newspaper, The National, which promised to bring a different type of journalism to the Middle East. Mohamed Khalaf Al Mazrouie, chairman of government-owned Abu Dhabi Media, notably said the newspaper was "born out of a vision that recognizes the key role that a free, professional and enlightened press plays in the national development process."[58] The launch of a paper espousing free speech principles in a country and region with heavily regulated media generated international publicity, including coverage in The New York Times and Columbia Journalism Review.[59] The original editor—a veteran leader of newspapers in Canada and the U.K.—was replaced after a little more than one year on the job by an Arabic-speaking, United States (U.S.) citizen deputy.[60] An academic study (performed by the author of this monograph) found that The National did bring a more professional style of journalism to Abu Dhabi, especially when compared to its Arabic-language competition, Al Ittihad.[61] The study found that the English-language newspaper did a far better job of practicing internationally accepted principles of journalism, such as verification of information, holding powerful institutions accountable, and operating as a voice for the voiceless. However, the study also found the same self-censorship as other media outlets. Examples of restrictions included typical "red lines" of coverage including a lack of reporting on actions of the security forces, avoidance of criticism of members of the royal families, and negative portrayal of business interests.

---

58. Editor, "The National, the UAE's New Quality English Newspaper, Launches in Abu Dhabi," *Media Middle East*, April 20, 2008, para. 4, Retrieved September 16, 2011, from http://mediame.com/news/announcement/the_national_the_uaes_new_quality_english_newspaper_launches_in_abu_dhabi.
59. Andrew Mills, "*A Vision in the Desert*," *Columbia Journalism Review*, May 22, 2009, http://www.cjr.org/feature/a_vision_in_the_desert.php; Heather Timmons, "*A New Mideast Paper Vows to Be Different*," *The New York Times*, April 29, 2008, sec. Business / Media & Advertising, http://www.nytimes.com/2008/04/29/business/media/29adcol.html?hp.
60. Liz Barrett, "*New Editor-in-Chief 'Appointed' For Abu Dhabi's National*," *Columbia Journalism Review*, accessed January 21, 2013, http://www.cjr.org/the_kicker/new_editorinchief_appointed_fo.php.
61. Matt Duffy, "Cultures of Journalism" in Arabic- and English-language Newspapers Within the United Arab Emirates,' *Journal of Middle East Media* 9, no. 1 (2013).

27. Three other major newspapers—Al Bayan, Emarat Al Youm and Emirates Business 24/7 (online only)—are owned by Dubai Media Incorporated, an arm of the Dubai government. The largest private newspapers are the English-language Khaleej Times (owned in part by government of Dubai) and Gulf News and the Arabic-language Al Khaleej.[62]

E. Concluding Remarks

28. The media environment in the UAE is robust, a reflection of the overall advanced level of development in the gulf country. The country enjoys a large number of media outlets—newspaper, radio, television, and the internet. However, the highly restrictive press environment limits the news media from operating in its internationally accepted role as a purveyor of information and a check to powerful government and business forces.

II. Infrastructure

A. Cable/Fiber-Optics Penetration

29. Cable penetration is only 14% in the UAE with many residents using illegal satellite receivers or opting for over-the-air alternatives. However, the country has invested heavily in the next generation of digital transmission, fiber-optic wire. Fiber-optic penetration is reportedly at 56% after a government-led push into that form of telecom infrastructure. Fiber-optic communications allow for internet speeds that far exceed cable lines while further blurring the distinction between television and internet transmissions since video can easily be streamed over such wide bandwidths.[63] The government-owned telecom firms, Etisalat and du, are the two cable and fiber-optic providers in the UAE.

B. Mobile Market

30. Mobile phones are incredibly popular in the UAE. Since many users have more than one phone, the official penetration rate for the UAE is 267%.[64] The government-owned telecom firms, Etisalat and du, are the only two mobile phone providers. Roughly 65% of the population owns a smartphone and several news outlets offer apps (for iPhone, Blackberry, or Android) to expand their reach.[65]

62. *UAE: Media Sustainability Index.*
63. *Arab Media Outlook 2011–2015.*
64. *Ibid.*
65. *Ibid.*

III. Technological and Economic Developments on the Media Markets

A. Digital Television

31. The UAE is slated to adopt digital television broadcasts in 2013. The switch from analog to digital television will allow far more channels and new interactive services on traditional over-the-air spectrums. Digital television also offers clearer pictures and audio and the ability to broadcast (over-the-air rather than via cable or fiber-optic) in high-definition. The government announced the switch from traditional broadcasting in 2011 but hasn't released any more information such as licensing regulations.[66]

B. Social Media and Digital Convergence

32. The UAE touts the highest penetration of smartphones in the world (73.8%).[67] Laptops also enjoy a high number of users at 78%. More than 90% of internet users in the UAE visit social media sites, with What's App (47%), Facebook (46%) and Skype (46%) being top applications.[68] Another social networking site, Google+, has gained in popularity despite its recent debut and is particularly popular with Emiratis. Video-sharing site YouTube is visited by 76% of internet users. Far more Emiratis (85%) prefer to browse the internet in Arabic rather than English.[69] The government updated its cybercrime law in 2012, in a move many saw as an attempt to rein in social media speech critical of the government.[70]

§3. Sources of Media Law

33. The sources of Media Law in the UAE derive from the Constitution, the 1980 Press and Publications Act, the NMC Resolution of 2010, the Penal Code, the Telecommunications Act, and the Cybercrime Law. Each of these elements will be discussed below.

I. Constitution

34. The UAE Constitution contains no explicit provisions related to protection for the news media. Article 30 does guarantee freedom of expression within limits of

66. Shane McGinley, "*UAE's Switch to Digital May Spark TV Boom, Says Regulator - Media - ArabianBusiness.com*," *Arabian Business*, April 26, 2011, http://www.arabianbusiness.com/uae-s-switch-digital-may-spark-tv-boom-says-regulator-396224.html.
67. https://en.wikipedia.org/wiki/List_of_countries_by_smartphone_penetration.
68. http://www.statista.com/statistics/284504/united-arab-emirates-social-network-penetration/.
69. *Ibid.*
70. Michael Peel, Camilla Hall in Abu Dhabi, and Abeer Allam in Cairo, "*UAE Cracks down on Internet Dissent*," *Financial Times*, November 13, 2012, http://www.ft.com/intl/cms/s/0/243afa46-2da9-11e2-9988-00144feabdc0.html#axzz2Id9h7YNH.

the law. And Article 31 guarantees freedom of communication via "post, telegraph, or other means of communication." The latter description could apply to newspapers and other forms of media but does not explicitly mention "the press" or journalists. The UAE Constitution can be found on the website for the UAE Cabinet, a group consisting of the ministers of the federal ministries.[71]

II. Legislation

35.

(1) Federal Law No.3 (as amended in 1987): UAE Penal Code.[72] The articles dealing with defamation have a palpable influence on the media landscape. Other articles prohibit insulting the country's rulers and publishing information about private individuals. (*See* relevant articles in Appendix 2.)[73]

(2) Federal Law No.15 of 1980: Press and Publications Act. The statute contains a large number of regulations on the media including ownership, prohibited types of reporting, and defamation. (*See* Appendix 3.)[74]

(3) Federal Law No.5 of 2012: Cybercrime Law. The statute contains a wide assortment of prohibitions for digital communications (which would apply to news websites and social media) such as the prohibition of sarcasm or anything that could damage the rulers' reputation or any communication that could upset the public order. (*See* relevant articles in Appendix 4.)[75]

III. National Media Council Chairman's Resolution

36. In 2010, after a draft revision to the 1980 Media Law was widely criticized and ultimately shelved, the NMC's chairman sent a 'Resolution of the Chairman of the Council Regarding the Media Content Criterion' to media outlets in the UAE. The document is notably absent on the NMC's website and has not been released widely in English nor publicly discussed after its release. (*See* Appendix 4.)[76]

---

71. http://www.uaecabinet.ae/English/UAEGovern 35. Three federal statutes (listed below) are most applicable to the media in UAE. Latter sections of this book expound upon each of the three laws: the Penal Code (as amended in 1987), the Press and Publications Act of 1980, and the Cybercrime Law of 2012. Copies of the penal code and cybercrime law can't be found easily on any government website. *See* Appendix 2 for the penal code excerpts that pertain to defamation and Appendix 5 for the cybercrime law excerpts that affect communication.
72. The penal code was amended again in 2005 but no changes applying to communication were enacted.
73. *See* appendix 2.
74. *See* appendix 3.
75. *See* appendix 5.
76. *See* appendix 4.

IV. Ethical Codes

37. The UAE Journalists Association is the professional trade group for reporters and editors in the country. In 2007, after the ruler of Dubai ordered that journalists should not be jailed for doing their job, the Journalists Association passed a Code of Ethics (*see* Appendix 6). Seven editors-in-chief from local newspapers and publication signed on to the document.[77]

38. With a few exceptions, the code of ethics reflects the best practices of the international journalism community including commitments to accuracy, independence, confidentiality of sources, and employing legitimate methods of news collection. However, in practice one of the norms in the code is not strictly followed. Number 26 of the ethics code reads: "Accepting valuable cash and kind gifts may cause a journalist to be biased in his coverage and is considered breach of the code." Many journalists and other observers in the UAE have documented first-hand accounts of bribery within newsrooms. Despite the code of ethics, many journalists accept money and gifts in exchange for positive coverage of businesses or government agencies.[78] Government officials reportedly give journalists cash or gifts (referred to as '*makroma*' in local parlance) including parcels of land in exchange for positive coverage. Observers noted that the exchange of '*makroma*' was particularly prevalent for UAE citizens who worked as journalists. Other observers have reported businesses that give monthly payments to journalists in exchange for coverage.[79] According to the NMC, these unethical practices are not permitted.[80]

77. "UAE Newspaper Editors Sign New Code of Ethics," *International Journalists Network*, November 10, 2007, http://ijnet.org/opportunities/uae-newspaper-editors-sign-new-code-ethics.
78. Matt Duffy, "Journalists Should Never Compromise on Integrity," *Gulf News*, March 9, 2012, http://gulfnews.com/opinions/columnists/journalists-should-never-compromise-on-integrity-1.991869.
79. Ahmed Mansoor, *United Arab Emirates: Media Sustainability Index* (Washington, D.C.: Irex, 2008).
80. Peter Hellyer, Personal Communication, email, March 12, 2013.

Part I. Freedom of Speech

§1. Constitutional Framework

39. The UAE Constitution does not explicitly guarantee freedom of the press. However, Articles 30 and 31 do guarantee freedom of expression:

> Article 30 Constitution
>
> Freedom of opinion and expressing it verbally, in writing or by other means of expression shall be guaranteed within the limits of law.
>
> Article 31 Constitution
>
> Freedom of communication by post, telegraph or other means of communication and the secrecy thereof shall be guaranteed in accordance with law.[81]

40. With the phrase "in writing or by other means of expression," Article 30 implies a freedom that extends to the press. Similarly, the language in Article 31 regarding "other means of communication" appears to include the press as well. But neither article specifically mention the press as a protected institution. Also, both articles contain the caveat that any freedom of expression exists only within the limits of law. The impact of this restriction regarding legal limits should not be overstated. Countries with strong protections for press freedoms either contain clauses in their constitutions that specifically allow for criminalization of some press actions (e.g., Belgium) or their courts have ruled to restrict the press in some way (defamation, national security) despite constitutional prohibitions (e.g., the United States.) However, the forthcoming examination of laws and regulations in the UAE shows that the limits on expression are quite abundant, regardless of the constitutional guarantees.

41. This book will examine some of the restrictions of UAE media and speech from an international perspective. A useful starting point for any discussion about ideal boundaries for freedom of the press and expression is the International Covenant on Civil and Political Rights (ICCPR), an international treaty created by the United Nations. The treaty outlines the competing societal interests for maintaining freedom of expression while acknowledging some limits that must be upheld. Section 19 reads:

81. *UAE Constitution.*

(1) Everyone shall have the right to hold opinions without interference.
(2) Everyone shall have the right to freedom of expression; this right shall include freedom to seek, receive and impart information and ideas of all kinds, regardless of frontiers, either orally, in writing or in print, in the form of art, or through any other media of his choice.
(3) The exercise of the rights provided for in paragraph 2 of this article carries with it special duties and responsibilities. It may therefore be subject to certain restrictions, but these shall only be such as are provided by law and are necessary:

(a) For respect of the rights or reputations of others;
(b) For the protection of national security or of public order or of public health or morals.[82]

42. The normative media environment envisioned by the ICCPR guarantees the right to free expression but concedes that no society can function without some limits. These restrictions are specific and narrow, including just five areas: rights of others, reputation management, national security, public order, and public health. Countries that feature strong protections for the press tend to follow the ICCPR approach with narrowly tailored curbs on speech that are carefully weighed to ensure political speech is not unduly restricted.

§2. Limitations of Constitutional Protection

43. The scope of constitutional Articles 30 and 31 to protect freedom of speech in the UAE is quite limited. Several laws severely limit freedom of expression and freedom of the press. The courts have not attempted to mitigate or balance the effect of these laws on freedom of expression. Given the lack of judicial independence, judges in matters involving the press seldom act against the wishes of the prosecutors. In no legal cases researched for this book did the author find an instance in which the judge referred to the constitutional protections for freedom of expression when weighing whether to uphold a criminal case against a journalist. For that matter, only one ruling in which a court sided with the defendant was uncovered. In that case, the security services have yet to release the acquitted party.[83]

44. Three laws have specifically affected freedom of the press—the 1987 Penal Code, the 1980 Press and Publications Act, and the 2012 Cybercrime Law. While none

82. *International Covenant on Civil and Political Rights* (Office of the United Nations High Commissioner for Human Rights, 1966), sec. 19, http://www.ohchr.org/EN/ProfessionalInterest/Pages/CCPR.aspx.
83. In a 2007 case involving defamation against two reporters for the *Khaleej Times*, an appeals court sided with the journalists. But, the ruling came *after* the ruler of Dubai declared that he didn't think journalists should go to jail for doing their jobs. In 2013, an Emirati who spoke critically of the lack of freedom of speech in the UAE was found not guilty. But, he was never released and remains imprisoned, presumably at the hands of the state security services. *See* Case Studies, Section V.

of these laws provide directly for prior restraint, the result is an environment in which journalists self-censor much of their work because of potential penalties.

45. In a 2011 interview with the CNN news channel, Shiekh Mohammed bin Rashid, the ruler of Dubai and vice-president and prime minister of the UAE, was asked about freedom of expression in his country. The interviewer noted that several activists had been arrested for their speech and that observers believed that the press and the people "cannot really say everything that they really think."[84] He responded:

> As long as they don't say something wrong about a person or whatever it is, they can say whatever they want. As I told you, we are not perfect. We are still learning. We are trying to do our job right and we're trying to help our own people … . We have our own democracy. You cannot transport your democracy to us—we are different. For example, our democracy comes from the Koran. As long as journalists don't step on somebody else, then you are free do what you like.[85]

46. His remarks show the importance placed upon not harming others in the process of written or spoken communication. This priority can be seen in much of the country's application of media and communication laws.

47. The result of these laws and other factors leave many observers to conclude that the freedom of speech and of the press in the UAE is severely restricted. In its 2015 last annual survey, the U.S. democracy advocacy group Freedom House ranked the country's press as "not free."[86] The French press freedom organization Reporters Without Borders ranked the country at 112 out of 176 countries.[87]

48. This view of a stifled speech and media environment is shared by some inside the country including Emirati Professor Dr. Abdulkhaleq Abdulla who suggested in Dubai's Gulf News that the "embarrassing" 2011 press freedom ranking should be "rectified through a concerted national effort."[88] Interestingly, the country's current minister of state for foreign affairs spoke frankly on the need for Arab media reform prior to his appointment. Speaking while a professor of political science at UAE University, Dr. Anwar Gargash told a media conference in 2005: "The Arab media is still very much state-owned and state-controlled. The way forward is to break the chains of the media."[89] And Emirati public affairs commentator Mishaal al Gergawi made the following recommendation in a 2011 Gulf News column:

---

84. Matt Duffy, 'CNN Asks UAE Leader About Freedom of Speech, Press,' *Www.mattjduffy.com*, December 6, 2011, para. 4, http://mattjduffy.com/2011/12/cnn-free-speech-interview/.
85. *Ibid.*, para. 5.
86. *Freedom in the World: United Arab Emirates* (Washington, D.C.: Freedom House, 2015), http://www.freedomhouse.org/report/freedom-world/2015/united-arab-emirates.
87. *2013 World Press Freedom Index: Dashed Hopes after Spring* (Paris, France: Reporters Without Borders), accessed February 6, 2013, http://en.rsf.org/press-freedom-index-2013,1054.html.
88. Abdulla Abdulkhaleq, "Ups and Downs of UAE Rankings," *Gulf News*, March 6, 2012, para. 12, http://gulfnews.com/opinions/columnists/ups-and-downs-of-uae-rankings-1.990500.
89. Lawrence Pintak, *The New Arab Journalist: Mission and Identity in a Time of Turmoil* (I. B. Tauris, 2011), 356.

> Liberate the local media: There is so much that is miscommunicated by foreign media just because the local media can't discuss it at the level of granularity that the former can. This allows for the loss of much of the situation's nuances.[90]

He spoke to a common complaint among residents of the UAE: Often the best place to go for news about certain subjects is foreign media outlets since the local media tends to steer away from discussing any 'sensitive stories'. The results are news stories that can miss key details or perspectives because the authors are expatriate journalists who may have limited knowledge of conditions in the country.

49. The government's media regulatory body flatly rejects claims that the media environment is stifled. In response to a Human Rights Watch (HRW) report critical of free expression in the UAE, the NMC issued a rebuttal that stated that journalists in the UAE "enjoy complete freedom in conveying the public opinion to the officials with the required objectivity and after verifying the facts."[91] The director-general of the NMC said that the press cannot be "absolutely free and irresponsible."[92]

§3. Spectrum of A Priori Censorship

50. The media is heavily regulated in the UAE, however in principle, there is no a priori censorship—prior restraint before publication. The concept of prior restraint—in which government official tells a private publisher not to publish a specific item—has long been derided as incompatible with free expression.[93]

51. The countries laws and regulations provide a large number of prohibitions for the media, although no directive allows specifically for prior restraint. The 1980 Press and Publication Act, the Penal Code as amended in 1987, the 2010 NMC Resolution, and Cybercrime Law of 2012 all regulate the media. The 1980 Press and Publications Act, in particular, contains 108 articles that regulate all forms of media in the UAE. After debate surrounding a revised Press Law ended without action, the NMC quietly issued a resolution from the chairman in 2010 that explicitly stated the 1980 law was still in force, noting several prohibitions that journalists should particularly

90. Mishaal Al Gergawi, "Incommunicado: The State of the Gulf," *Gulf News*, April 17, 2011, para. 11, http://gulfnews.com/opinions/columnists/incommunicado-the-state-of-the-gulf-1.794063#.UO7euwvQJQQ.twitter.
91. *Journalists and Writers Associations Slam HRW Report* (Abu Dhabi, UAE: Emirates News Agency (WAM), January 27, 2011), http://www.uaeinteract.com/docs/Journalists_and_writers_associations_slam_HRW_report_/44235.htm.
92. Abdullah Rasheed, "Freedom and Responsibility Go Together to Secure State's Interest," *Gulf News*, February 22, 2011, para. 7, http://gulfnews.com/news/gulf/uae/media/freedom-and-responsibility-go-together-to-secure-state-s-interest-1.765596.
93. *See* , for instance, John Milton, *Aeropagitica: A Speech for the Liberty of Unlicensed Printing to the Parliament of England* (Forgotten Books, 2008).

abide, and clarifying that the law applied to all "audio" and "visual" media in addition to the laws stated regulation of newspapers and film.

52. Despite no formal mechanisms, the UAE has developed an efficient system that effectively creates a priori censorship over a wide variety of information. Observers in the UAE and wider Arab world refer to the informal boundaries of reporting as "red lines" that journalists adopt and understand. For instance, the NMC also operates the official news agency of the government, the Emirates News Agency (known by its Arabic-language abbreviation, WAM). Often the newspapers wait for the news agency to report on "sensitive issues" (such as security-related arrests or an incident involving a member of the ruling family) before broaching a story. If the WAM news agency ignores a story, then editors often follow their lead and avoid the stories in their newspapers.[94] Journalists—many of whom are well-paid expatriates in the country on a work visa—worry that violating this accepted practice could lead to loss of a job, deportation, or even jail.[95] This informal system effectively gives the NMC a priori censorship without having a government official in every media outlet newsroom.[96] A good example of the adoption of "red lines" involved a 2014 story in the International New York Times about the poor treatment of laborers at the NYU Abu Dhabi campus. On the day of publication, the local printer decided against publishing the entire paper. The Khaleej Times announced that the newspaper would not be published that day because it was deemed "too sensitive for local printing."[97] The printer is owned in part by the ruler of Dubai, the prime minister of the country. The environment allows the government to effectively issue prior restraint without officially using the legal system.

53. The Media Law does give the government the power to broadly engage in prior restraint by closing newspapers altogether for a certain length of time.[98] Article 98 of the 1980 Press and Publication Act allows for suspension of newspaper publishing for a period of up to one year if the press:

> defames Islamic beliefs or incites hatred against the system of ruling, or causes harm to the supreme interests of the country, or publishes materials that cause damage to the constitution, particularly to the concept of unity and federation, or threatens public order, or serves foreign interests that contradict national interests.[99]

94. Duffy, "'Cultures of Journalism'" in Arabic- and English-language Newspapers Within the United Arab Emirates"; Matt Duffy, "Newspapers Inconsistent over Activist Arrests," *Mideastposts.com*, April 12, 2011, http://mideastposts.com/2011/04/12/uae-press-inconsistent-over-handling-of-blogger-arrests/.
95. Dana El-Baltaji, "Emirates Press Law," *Arab Media & Society*, Fall 2009, http://www.arabmediasociety.com/?article=727.
96. Many observers strongly suspect that the government engaged in prior restraint related to allegations of torture against a member of the Abu Dhabi ruling family. *See* the case study on Shiekh Issa bin Zayed al Nahyan in Chapter 3, section 10, for more information.
97. http://america.aljazeera.com/articles/2014/5/20/nytimes-uae-nyu.html; http://www.newsweek.com/uae-halts-printing-new-york-times-over-damning-nyu-labor-article-251495.
98. Legal scholars may debate whether such closure meets the definition of prior restraint, a concept that generally refers to the restriction of a specific piece of information, not everything an outlet may publish.
99. *UAE: 1980 Press and Publications Act*, 1980, nmc.gov.ae/en/MediaLawsAndRegulation/4.pdf.

The article allows the minister of the now-defunct Information and Culture ministry to shut down a news outlet for up to two weeks.[100] To close a media outlet for a longer period of time requires the approval of the UAE Cabinet. The courts closed the Arabic-language newspaper Emarat al Youm (Emirates Today) for twenty days in 2007 following a report tied to the royal family of Abu Dhabi was determined to be defamatory (*see* Chapter 3, Case Studies, for more details.)[101]

§4. Spectrum of A Posteriori Restrictive Measures

54. The Penal Code, 1980 Press and Publications Act, and 2012 Cybercrime Law allow a wide range of penalties for violating a litany of prohibitions for journalists operating in the UAE. Many observers have noted that these a posteriori restrictions conflict with the ability of journalists to perform their societal duties to report critically and convey news and information.[102]

I. Penal Code

55. The Penal Code, Federal Law No. 3 of 1987, provides stiff penalties for the press in cases of defamation including jail and fines.[103] The law provides little protection for reporting including no clear exception for the truth of the information disseminated. (*See* Chapter 3, "Journalists Liabilities," section 1, for a full discussion of the country's slander and libel laws.)

56. Articles 8 and 176 of the UAE Penal Code make it a crime to publicly insult the rulers of the UAE. The law was used in 2011 to prosecute several online activists for statements made on a website during a period of upheaval across the region.[104]

57. Article 263 of the Penal Code mandates a fine or imprisonment for anyone "who publishes, through any means of publicity," any material that influences a judge in a court case. It also prohibits publication of anything with the "intention of hindering a person from declaring any information to the competent authorities, or of influencing the public opinion in favor of or against any of the parties in a case or investigation." The provision regarding influencing public opinion may affect the media's approach toward naming criminal suspects (*See* Chapter 3, section 9.) The article provides for a harsher punishment if the published material turns out to be false.

---

100. The authority shifts to the National Media Council, the regulatory agency formed in 2006.
101. RWB, *Authorities Bend Rules to Block Access to Online Magazine - Reporters Without Borders*, para. 1.
102. Abdulkhaleq, "Ups and Downs of UAE Rankings"; Abdullah Rasheed, "The Ceiling of Press Freedom in UAE Is Falling," *Gulf News*, March 2, 2010, http://gulfnews.com/opinions/columnists/the-ceiling-of-press-freedom-in-uae-is-falling-1.590497; Matt Duffy, "Challenges Facing Press Freedom," *Gulf News*, February 10, 2012, http://gulfnews.com/opinions/columnists/challenges-facing-press-freedom-1.978338.
103. The penal code was also amended in 2005, but the sections that potentially relate to media laws and journalism were changed in 1987.
104. *UAE: End "travesty of Justice" for Five Convicted over President Insults | Amnesty International.*

58. Article 264 of the Penal Code provides for several types of information that cannot be published:

(1) Information concerning a current investigation of a case of any documents if the criminal justice authority has prohibited it.
(2) Information regarding investigations related to kinship, marriage, guardianship, divorce, alimony, separation, adultery, slander, or divulgence of secrets.
(3) Names or pictures of accused juvenile delinquents.
(4) Names or pictures of victims in crimes committed against honor.
(5) Names or pictures of convicts with stay of execution of the punishment.
(6) Deliberations of courts and tribunals.
(7) Information concerning the cases which the courts have decided to try in secret session or have prohibited from their publication.

59. The penalty for violating the prohibitions is up to one year of imprisonment and a fine of up to United Arab Emirates Dirhams (AED) 10,000 (USD 2,700).

60. Article 265 of the Penal Code appears to prohibit publishing information that inaccurately reflects the events in open court. The exact wording of the law criminalizes "any individual who, with his honesty and in bad faith publishes, through any means of publicity, what has taken place during the hearings in open court."[105] The penalty for such a violation also up to one year of imprisonment and a fine of up to AED 10,000 (USD 2,700).

61. The Penal Code also prohibits the blasphemy of Islam and other religions. Article 312 allows for jail and a fine for anyone found to abuse "any sacred or holy Islamic rites" or "blaspheming any of the divine recognized religions."[106] These articles could conceivably be used against a journalist who addressed religion in a manner deemed to be offensive. (*See* Chapter 3, section 4 for more on blasphemy.)

62. Article 378 of the Penal Code provide penalties to anyone who "through any means of publicity, publishes news, pictures or comments pertaining to the secrets of the people's private or familial lives even if such publications are real and true."[107] A journalist violating this law would face up to one year in prison and/or an AED 10,000 (USD 2,700) fine.

63. Article 372 of the Penal Code criminalizes publishing material that causes "moral harm."[108] The broad prohibition could be applied to a wide variety of material. A journalist violating this law could face two years and prison and a fine of up to AED 20,000 (USD 5,400).

105. *UAE Penal Code*, 1987, http://www.scribd.com/doc/122309224/UAE-Penal-Code-amended-1987.
106. *Ibid.*
107. *Privacy Issues: Statutory Rules on Privacy*, Report: United Arab Emirates (London: Privacy International), accessed December 7, 2012, https://www.privacyinternational.org/reports/united-arab-emirates/ii-privacy-issues.
108. Patti McCracken, *Insult Laws: Insulting to Press Freedom* (World Press Freedom Committee, 2010), http://www.freedomhouse.org/sites/default/files/Insult%20Law%20Report.pdf.

II. The 1980 Press and Publications Act

64. The 1980 Press and Publications Act details a far more expansive list of prohibitions for journalists. The following is a description of each restriction in the Media Law:

- No criticism of head of state of rulers of the individual emirates (Article 70).
- No work that involves instigation against Islam, the ruling system, or anything that causes harm to the interest of the state (Article 71).
- No opinions that violate public discipline and order, involve insult to teenagers, or circulate subversive ideas (Article 72).
- Nothing that promotes criminal activity, incitement of hatred, or encourage dissension among individuals of society (Article 73).
- No confidential official or military communications (Article 74).
- No distorted descriptions of meetings, deliberations, or court hearings (Article 75).
- Nothing that blemishes the president of an Arab, Islamic or any other friendly state or anything that causes strife between the UAE and other Arab, Islamic, and friendly countries (Article 76).
- Nothing that defames Arabs or their civilization and heritage (Article 77).
- No court proceedings if the presiding judge so decrees (Article 78).
- No details of private life if publication meant to disgrace individual. No publication of private information for purpose of extortion (Article 79).
- No false news about individuals (Article 80).
- Nothing that could cause harm to national currency or national economy. (Article 81).
- No publications or advertisements that include any phrases, expressions or pictures that are inconsistent with public conduct, or otherwise mislead public (Article 82).
- No advertisements on medicines or pharmaceutical preparations unless approved by Ministry of Health (Article 83).
- No maligning of public officials unless writer can prove he did so "in good faith" (Article 84).
- No reporting without multiple points of view (Article 85).

65. Penalties for violations of the 1980 Press and Publications Act can reach up to a fine of AED 20,000 (USD 5,400), imprisonment for up to two years, and the publication's closure for up to two months.

66. Some parts of the law appear to go unenforced. For instance, Article 76 prohibits blemishing the president of an Arab, Islamic, or any other friendly state and Article 77 bans the defamation of Arabs and their civilization. Given these broad declarations, reporting on the abuses of leaders in Syria, Libya, and Egypt are at odds with the Media Law. Local media did cover the events diligently.

67. Observers have noted that many of these provisions put overly broad restrictions on the press, leading to inevitable self-censorship.[109] For instance, Article 81 prohibits publication of news that "causes damage to the national economy." Given this ambiguous mandate, reporting on negative business news could potentially lead to criminal charges. Article 84 offers perhaps the broadest declaration. The article prohibits reporters from "maligning a public official" or anyone "assigned to perform a public job." A journalist exposing corruption in a government agency could easily violate the letter of this law—even if the report is accurate. The article does provide a provision allowing for maligning if done in "good faith," but the term is nebulous and no provision explicitly states that truth of the report provides exoneration. Truth as a defense for defamation is an internationally accepted principle in countries where the press is not unduly restrained. (*See* Chapter 3, section 1, for a full discussion of the UAE's defamation laws.)

III. The 2010 Resolution on Media Regulation

68. In the wake of the debate over the Press Law, the NMC quietly issued a resolution regarding media regulation in the UAE.[110] The document was apparently given to the media outlets in the UAE but never publicized widely—it cannot be found on the government news agency website nor did any press outlet report on the seemingly major policy announcement. The resolution from the NMC chair looks similar to a law, containing five articles each with its own set of rules.

69. Article 1 restates that the 1980 Press and Publications Law is still the main source of media regulation in the country. The document also states that the original 1980 law applies to media outlets in the media free zone areas in Dubai, Abu Dhabi, and Ra's al-Khaimah. The specific application of the 1980 law to entities in the free zone provides clarity on a previously unclear issue.

70. Article 1 also states that the 1980 Media Law applies to "visible, audible, and legible" media in the UAE. The original law did not specify any media outside of newspapers and film, so the new directive means the Press and Publication Law applies to both television and the Internet in addition to the other media. In many countries, regulation of broadcast outlets such as radio and television are handled separately from print and Internet because of the difference in the media. (For a fuller discussion of this issue, *see* Part III: The NMC.)

71. Article 2 of the document reaffirms all of the 1980 Press Law but notes that media corporations should abide by several prohibitions 'particularly':

(1) To not abuse God, Islam, and any of the '*heavenly religions*.'
(2) To respect the 'regime system' in the UAE and its political symbols and corporations.
(3) To not abuse national unity and social solidarity nor ignite ideological or tribal issues.

109. El-Baltaji, "Emirates Press Law;" Duffy, "Challenges Facing Press Freedom"; Mansoor, *United Arab Emirates: Media Sustainability Index.*
110. *Resolution of the Chairman Regarding the Media Content Criterion.*

(4) To respect the trends and policies adopted by the United Arab Emirates at the local level and the level of its relations with other countries.
(5) To not abuse the economical system of the state and to not "disseminate misleading and tendentious rumors and news."[111]

72. Article 3 directs each media outlet to keep three months of records regarding publications and broadcasts ready for inspection from the NMC. The article also mandates that media producers provide prompt replies to all matters given by the NMC in response to complaints reported by the public or any other party.

73. Article 4 outlines the various punishments the NMC may exact upon violators. Penalties include a warning, a written apology, a suspension of publication license, or the complete cancellation of the license.[112] The article states clearly that these penalties will not supersede other punishments in other laws (such as the Penal Code which provides jail and fines for defamation.)

74. This NMC resolution was never released to the public. Therefore, no journalists or outside organizations debated its merits. However, the same criticisms that applied to the draft Press Law and the Standing Law of 1980 would apply to this directive. Much of the instructions are overly broad. For instance, the edict to "respect the trends and policies adopted by the United Arab Emirates" could easily to lead to self-censorship. A journalist interviewing a citizen who disagreed with a policy of the UAE could conceivably be breaking the law. The directive prohibiting abusing the economic system or spreading tendentious (i.e., one-sided) news is also overly broad and subjective.

IV. Cybercrime Law of 2012

75. The updated Cybercrime Law of 2012 also affords penalties for any journalists with an online presence as well as anyone using social media.[113] The law provides for the following prohibitions, some of which overlap with the Penal Code and Media Law:

- Transmitting, publishing or promoting pornographic material, gambling activities, and any other indecent acts (Article 17).
- Publishing news, electronic photographs or photographs or scenes, comments, data and information even if they are authentic (Article 21).
- Publishing any programs or ideas that would promote disorder, hate, racism, or sectarianism and damage national unity or social peace or damage public order and public decency (Article 24).

111. *Ibid.*, para. 14.
112. In an email exchange with the author, an official with the National Media Council indicated that no further "decisions" had been issued since 2010.
113. *UAE Cybercrime Law of 2012*, 2012, http://www.scribd.com/doc/120536757/UAE-Cybercrime-Law-of-2012.

- Publishing any information, news, caricatures, or any other kind of pictures that would pose threats to the security of the state and to its highest interests or violate its public order (Article 28).
- Publishing anything to deride or to damage the reputation or the stature of the state or any of its institutions, its president, the vice-president, any of the rulers of the Emirates, their crown princes, the deputy rulers, the national flag, the national anthem, the emblem of the state or any of its symbols (Article 29).
- Publishing anything that calls for the overthrow of the system of government of the state or to seize it, or to seek to disrupt the Constitution or the effective laws of the state, or to oppose the basic principles that constitute the foundations of the system of government of the state (Article 30).
- Publishing any call for demonstrations, marches and similar activities without a license being obtained in advance from the competent authorities (Article 32).
- Publishing any misleading, inaccurate or incorrect information that would damage the interests of the state or damage its reputation and stature (Article 38).
- Publishing any call to disobey the laws and regulations of the state that may be in effect (Article 47).[114]

76. Penalties for these crimes include fines, imprisonment and deportation (for foreigners). Many observers have noted that these prohibitions are overly broad and would likely lead to self-censorship both from online journalists and any resident using social media in the UAE.[115] The government updated the cybercrime law at a time of increased anxiety over instability in the region. In the same year, security forces arrested more than ninety Emirati citizens on security grounds, many of whom had been expressing dissatisfaction with the rulers on social media networks.[116] (*See* section 6 below for a greater discussion of limits to freedom of expression via social media.)

77. This section details a litany of *posteriori* restrictive measures for the press in the UAE. The result is a profession that is defined by its restrictions, often unable to function in the traditionally defined beneficial role of the press in society.

V. Anti-terrorism Law of 2014

78. In summer 2014, the UAE passed an anti-terrorism law that provides charges for speech-related activities. Article 1 of the new law categorizes "antagonizing the state" as a form of terrorism. Article 14 sets the death penalty or life in prison to anyone who undermines "national unity of social peace." Article 15 makes it illegal to publicly declare a "lack of allegiance to the state." Later that year, the Federal Supreme Court

114. The preceding articles have been translated from Arabic. Specific phrasing may come from either Dubai's *Gulf News* or the UAE government's translation.
115. "UAE: Cybercrimes Decree Attacks Free Speech," *Human Rights Watch*, November 28, 2012, http://www.hrw.org/news/2012/11/28/uae-cybercrimes-decree-attacks-free-speech; 'Revisions to UAE Cybercrime Law Stifle Free Expression,' *Freedom House*, November 2012, http://www.freedomhouse.org/article/revisions-uae-cybercrime-law-stifle-free-expression.
116. Kenneth Katzman, *The United Arab Emirates (UAE): Issues for U.S. Policy* (Washington, D.C.: Congressional Research Service, October 4, 2012).

apparently used the new anti-terrorism law to sentence an Emirati to three years in prison.[117] Human rights groups widely criticized the law as an abridgment of freedom of expression.[118]

§5. Prior Authorization for Publishing

79. All press outlets in the UAE are mandated to receive a license before operating. Articles 31 through 36 of the Press and Publications Act of 1980 detail the exact requirements for obtaining and retaining a license to publish. It is unclear whether some smaller online news sites are operating without obtaining a license.

80. In many countries, newspapers have no special licensing requirements—apart from the same business licenses any firm must receive from a local authority.[119] Generally, this lack of licensing is thought to provide assurances that journalists will not be punished for critical reporting by authorities who can take away their licenses. However, most countries do license broadcast outlets because of the scarcity of television and radio spectrum as well as the public interest since the audio-visual medium is more pervasive than print. However, many countries provide statutory or judicial protection for the license granting and revocation process to assuage concerns of political retribution.[120]

§6. Restrictions of Speech During Regional Protests

81. At the beginning of 2011, the "Arab Spring" was well underway. Facilitated by social media sites such as YouTube, Facebook, and Twitter, Arab countries around the Middle East were protesting the status quo and calling for greater freedoms.[121] Tunisia and Egypt had already seen their long-standing rulers depart and Libya headed toward civil war. The UAE's regional ally Bahrain was also seeing regular protests as its population strafed against its rulers, a situation troubled further by sectarian differences. Bahrain's rulers are Sunni Muslims who oversee a majority Shiite population. In March 2011, both Saudi Arabia and the UAE sent forces into Bahrain to help quell the raging protests there.[122]

117. http://www.wam.ae/en/news/emirates/1395272976050.html.
118. https://www.hrw.org/news/2014/12/03/uae-terrorism-law-threatens-lives-liberty; http://muftah.org/antiterrorism-and-antitorture-in-the-uae/.
119. Steve Buckley et al., *Broadcasting, Voice, and Accountability: A Public Interest Approach to Policy, Law, and Regulation* (World Bank Publications, 2008).
120. Perry Keller, *European and International Media Law: Liberal Democracy, Trade, and the New Media* (Oxford University Press, 2011).
121. . Philip Howard, "*The Arab Spring's Cascading Effects*," *Miller-McCune*, February 23, 2011, https://psmag.com/economics/the-cascading-effects-of-the-arab-spring-28575.
122. Reem Khalifa, "*Saudis, Other Gulf Nations Send Force to Bahrain*," *The (U.K.) Guardian*, March 14, 2011, http://www.guardian.co.uk/world/feedarticle/9545419.

82. During this regional upheaval, about 130 Emiratis signed an online petition calling for political reforms in the UAE.[123] The petition sought to move the country toward a more democratic system via a larger, more representative and empowered FNC. At the time, only about 6,000 people voted in the previous FNC election, held in 2006. After the petition, the government did greatly enlarge the number of voters in the next FNC election, expanding the electoral college to roughly 129,000 people. The FNC remained without any legislative authority other than to deliberate and suggest changes to some laws.[124] Critics also complained that the electors to the FNC were hand-picked by the rulers of the seven Emirates—and notable figures were not included in the list.[125] As prescribed in the Constitution, half of the forty-member FNC were elected while the other half were appointed by the rulers of the Emirates. Only one woman was elected to the FNC, although several more were appointed.[126]

83. The government's reaction to the online petition calling for universal suffrage was quite deliberate. On 6 April, two of the country's oldest civil-society groups: the jurists and teachers associations issued press releases in which they called for greater democracy. Within a month, the government had dissolved the elected boards of both organizations and replaced them with appointees.[127]

84. The government arrested five Emiratis in April 2011 who had signed or supported the petition. They would later be referred to as the "UAE5."[128] All five had posted comments on an online discussion board, Al Hewer ("the dialogue"), that had been blocked by authorities earlier in the year. The government-owned telecom firms blocked access to the site by citing the government's online "prohibited content guidelines"; however, the site's content does not seem to fit into any of the categories.[129] The five were officially charged with "insulting the UAE's top leadership, endangering national security, and inciting people to protest."[130] After seven months in jail, the men were all convicted in a security court trial and received prison sentences of two to three years. The following day, the UAE's President Sheikh Khalifa bin Zayed pardoned the five men as part of the country's fortieth anniversary celebrations.[131] The local press offered muted coverage of the arrest and trial, although the English press tended

---

123. "The United Arab Emirates: Getting Twitchy About Democracy," *The Economist*, June 30, 2011, http://www.economist.com/node/18898137.
124. While the FNC is consulted on some laws, others are sometimes signed into law without any notice. The Cybercrime Law of 2012, for instance, was simply announced after the president issued a decree enacting the law.
125. Mahmoud Habboush, "*UAE Nationals Ask: Why Can't We All Vote?*," *Huffington Post*, September 21, 2011, http://www.huffingtonpost.com/2011/09/21/uae-nationals-ask-why-ca_n_973656.html.
126. Samir Salama & Bassma Al Jandaly, "*Shaikh Khalifa to Open New FNC Term*," *Gulf News*, November 15, 2011, http://gulfnews.com/news/gulf/uae/government/shaikh-khalifa-to-open-new-fnc-term-1.930855.
127. "The United Arab Emirates: Getting Twitchy About Democracy."
128. Angela Shah, "*United Arab Emirates Step Up Efforts to Counter Dissent*," *The New York Times*, May 30, 2012, sec. World / Middle East, http://www.nytimes.com/2012/05/31/world/middleeast/united-arab-emirates-step-up-efforts-to-counter-dissent.html.
129. "Prohibited Content Categories."
130. Surk, "5 UAE Convicted Reform Activists Freed from Jail," para. 2.
131. Surk, "5 UAE Convicted Reform Activists Freed from Jail."

to be more engaged than its Arabic counterpart.[132] Some observers thought the government took the action against the "UAE5" to send a message about the toleration for public dissent in the Emirates, particularly via electronic media.[133]

85. In 2012, the government took more action against people using social media sites such as Facebook and the micro-blogging site Twitter. Increasingly, Twitter effectively served the same role as Al Hewer, an online space for unencumbered public discussion.[134] Later that year, the UAE authorities made more arrests over online and social media speech. One Emirati was charged with using Twitter to "incite sedition" and "abuse religion."[135] Another activist was arrested and accused of insulting the ruler of the emirate of Sharjah after he discussed the mistreatment of expatriate laborers on Twitter.[136] One person who complained on Twitter about his experience with Dubai police was arrested for defamation of the police chief.[137] After spending two months in jail, the chief dropped the charges. The state news agency publicized most of these cases, signaling the government's desire to alert residents to the lines being drawn regarding speech on social media platforms.

86. International observers reported more than sixty Emiratis were arrested and indefinitely detained in 2012, although the government provided little transparency about the detentions. Some critics said the charges revolved around their posts on Twitter however the government did not release detailed information about each arrest.[138] In August 2012, the government news agency released a statement from Federal Cabinet defending the detentions. The government said that detainees were "conspiring against the state and had links to 'external elements'."[139] Many of the detainees were members of "Al Islah," a group linked with the larger Muslim Brotherhood movement that had recently taken power in Egypt following a revolution against thirty-two-year incumbent President Hosni Mubarak.[140] At least three of the detainees were lawyers, including one who had represented the "UAE5" in the previous year.[141] In fall 2012, the European Parliament issued a resolution condemning the arrests and the restrictions on freedom of expression in the UAE.[142] In early 2013, the government

132. Duffy, "Newspapers Inconsistent over Activist Arrests."
133. "UAE: Civil Society Crackdown Widens," *Human Rights Watch*, May 3, 2011, http://www.hrw.org/news/2011/05/03/uae-civil-society-crackdown-widens; Christopher M. Davidson, "*The Making of a Police State*," *Foreign Policy*, April 14, 2011, http://www.foreignpolicy.com/articles/2011/04/14/the_making_of_a_police_state.
134. Matt Duffy, "*Obstacles to Liberty*," *Index on Censorship* 41, no. 4 (December 1, 2012): 48–54, doi:10.1177/0306422012466798.
135. RWB, *Authorities Crack down on Social Networks and Activist Bloggers*, para. 3.
136. RWB, *Authorities Crack down on Social Networks and Activist Bloggers*.
137. Al Amir, "*Dubai Police Chief Defamed on Twitter, Court Hears*."
138. Jenifer Fenton, "*Crackdown on Islamists in the UAE*," *The Arabist*, August 4, 2012, http://arabist.net/blog/2012/8/4/crackdown-on-islamists-in-the-uae.html.
139. Zaid Sabah, "*Islamists in U.A.E Had Links With 'External Elements': WAM*," *Bloomberg*, August 12, 2012, http://www.bloomberg.com/news/2012-08-13/islamists-in-u-a-e-had-links-with-external-elements-wam.html.
140. Ola Salem, "*Islah 'Does Not Represent UAE Interests'*," *The National*, accessed May 9, 2013, http://www.thenational.ae/news/uae-news/islah-does-not-represent-uae-interests.
141. Fenton, "*Crackdown on Islamists in the UAE*."
142. Baltaji, "*U.A.E. 'Shocked' at EU Parliament Resolution on Human Rights*."

announced formally that more than ninety Emiratis would stand trial on charges of trying to "seize power."[143]

87. In November 2012, the government released an updated version of the Cybercrime Law of 2006. Many of the provisions of the updated law (*see* section 4 above) restrict online speech for both journalists and users of social media. For instance, one article of the law prohibits publishing anything that may deride or damage the "reputation or the stature of the state." Observers noted this broad prohibition and many others in the law could effectively make it illegal to utter any criticism of any policy of the UAE.[144] One organization said, "the decree's vaguely worded provisions provide a legal basis to prosecute and jail people who use information technology to, among other things, criticize senior officials, argue for political reform, or organize unlicensed demonstrations."

§7. Social, Political Regulation of the Internet

88. Internet websites are regularly blocked in the UAE when they are determined to contain information deemed unacceptable. The Telecommunications Regulatory Authority, a government agency created through Decree No.3 of 2003—Telecom Law, oversees the regulation of the Internet. The agency is tasked with ensuring adequate telecom services throughout the country and establishing a practical policy structure to carry out that mission.[145] The TRA is responsible for creating the Internet Access Management (IAM) policy that outlines the content that is prohibited for the country's two government-owned Internet Service Providers (ISPs): Etisalat and du.[146] The ISPs are required as part of their license to develop tools to ensure that these guidelines are followed. The IAM policy for the UAE includes the following thirteen prohibitions:

(1) Internet content that assists users in bypassing blocked content.
(2) Internet content that teaches criminal or unethical skills including downloading pirated software, music, and videos. Other prohibited acts include lessons on bomb-making, phreaking (breaking phone security or phone service theft), scams and fraud, terrorism, evading law enforcement, stalking, and lock picking.
(3) Internet content that provides for online dating or matchmaking, services that contradict "the ethics and morals of the UAE." Exemptions to this prohibition are chatting services, chatting groups and social networking, and forums.
(4) Internet content that provide "information on purchasing, manufacturing, promoting, and using illegal drugs."

143. "United Arab Emirates to Try 94 Accused of Trying to Seize Power," *CNN*, January 27, 2013, http://www.cnn.com/2013/01/27/world/meast/uae-plot.
144. "UAE: Cybercrimes Decree Attacks Free Speech."
145. "About TRA," *Telecommunications Regulatory Authority (TRA)*, accessed May 9, 2013, http://www.tra.gov.ae/about_tra.php.
146. 'TRA Issues Regulations Policy on 'Internet Access Management',' *UAE Interact*, February 8, 2008, http://www.uaeinteract.com/docs/TRA_issues_regulation_policy_on_Internet_Access_Management/31367.htm.

(5) Internet content containing nudity or pornography. This ban applies to stories, jokes, animations and video. The prohibition also extends to sites which promote distribution of such content such as peer-to-peer websites.
(6) Internet content that promotes or enables gambling including links, tips, sports picks, lottery results, and horse, car or boat racing.
(7) Internet content that provides information and tools for hacking that help individuals gain unauthorized access to computer systems. However, "ethical hacking" is exempted.
(8) Internet content that contains material that "expresses hate to religions."
(9) Internet content that fraudulently obtains confidential information while posing as a legitimate business.
(10) Internet content that contains spyware, software that gains private information without the users' knowledge.
(11) Internet content that provides unlicensed Voice over Internet Protocol (VoIP) service that allows users to make phone calls by using their Internet connection.
(12) Internet content that provides information that supports terrorism including material training or funding of terrorist groups.
(13) Internet content under top-level domain, domains' names that offend "against, is objectionable to, or is contrary to the public interest, public morality, public order, public and national security, Islam morality or is otherwise prohibited by any applicable UAE law, regulation, procedure, order or requirement."[147]

89. The advocacy group OpenNet noted the final prohibition allows for the blocking of Israel's domain name, .il.[148] Like all other Gulf countries, the UAE does not formally recognize Israel's existence.[149] However, anecdotal evidence suggests the.il domain name—which was blocked at the time of OpenNet's report—is no longer blocked.

90. The ISPs, government-owned telecom companies Etisalat and du, handle the blocking of websites containing prohibited content. Occasionally, Internet sites may be blocked on one ISP but not on the other.[150] A website form allows users to flag material as prohibited and the ISPs tend to block content immediately based on a complaint. However both sites have systems for requesting the block be removed—assuming the website does not fit into any of the thirteen categories.[151]

91. In 2009, the chief of Dubai's police force once called for the video-sharing website YouTube to be blocked in the UAE because it contained videos that "incites

147. "Prohibited Content Categories," *Etisalat*, accessed June 23, 2012, http://www.etisalat.ae/assets/document/blockcontent.pdf.
148. "United Arab Emirates: OpenNet Initiative."
149. "International Recognition of Israel," *Jewish Virtual Library*, accessed May 9, 2013, http://www.jewishvirtuallibrary.org/jsource/Peace/recogIsrael.html.
150. "Etisalat Blocks Skype. Du Doesn't. And Neither Blocks Chatroulette. Confusing, Huh?," *Kippreport.com*, March 18, 2010, http://www.kippreport.com/blog/kipps-blog/etisalat-blocks-skype-du-doesn%e2%80%99t-and-neither-blocks-chatroulette-confusing-huh/.
151. "About Us - Blocking and Unblocking Internet Content," *Etisalat*, accessed May 10, 2013, http://www.etisalat.ae/eportal/en/corporate/blocking-unblocking.html.

hatred."[152] Lt. Gen. Dhahi Khalfan Tamim said the site contained videos that "sparked dissension," especially on religious beliefs. "Publishing pornographic material and defamatory ideas is not freedom," Tamim wrote in the Arabic newspaper Emarat Al Youm.[153] The site was not blocked completely but individual videos are sometimes blocked in keeping with the prohibited content guidelines.[154]

92. A 2009 report by OpenNet Initiative found some websites related to political or religious themes to be blocked. For example, UAEprison.com, a site hosting testimonials from prisoners and human rights critiques of the UAE, was blocked. Other sites that centered on human rights abuses or unflattering portraits of life in the UAE were also blocked despite the fact that these sites do not appear to violate any of the prohibited content criteria.[155] OpenNet also found that sites that criticized the local economy were also blocked such as one site that accused government officials of misleading the public about the state of the economy during the Dubai financial crisis in 2008.[156]

93. Other sites that were blocked included information that opposed or presented unorthodox approaches to Islam, including the UAE-based Lands of Sands.[157] In a column about bloggers who pushed the boundaries of acceptable opinion writing in the Gulf, Emirati commentator Sultan Al Qassemi noted that a "self-confessed Emirati atheist" who went by the penname Ahmed Benkerishan, authored the blog.[158] The topics of Benkerishan's last blog entries were as diverse as sex and political Islam. Al Qassemi noted:

> Although the Land of Sands was not necessarily a political blog, Benkerishan criticized the use of religion in politics, using what I suspect religiously inclined individuals would deem as highly offensive cartoons. These included many that would mock religion and depict God ordering adherents to obey him.[159]

94. OpenNet noted that three of Benkerishan's blog sites were blocked in the UAE. The report also noted that sites that promoted minority faiths were also blocked.[160] The OpenNet research also found that sites on Nazism, Holocaust denial and other anti-Semitic sites were also blocked.[161]

95. At times the TRA will instruct that the individual ISPs to block a specific site. Such a move came in 2009 in response to a cartoon series that contained material

152. "Call to Blank Out YouTube in Emirates Too," *Khaleej Times*, March 10, 2009, para. 1, http://www.khaleejtimes.com/DisplayArticleNew.asp? col=&section=theuae&xfile=data/theuae/2009/March/theuae_March239.xml.
153. *Ibid.*, para. 4.
154. "United Arab Emirates: OpenNet Initiative."
155. *Ibid.*
156. *Ibid.*
157. *Ibid.*
158. Sultan Al-Qassemi, "*Pioneer Bloggers in the Gulf Arab States*," *Jadaliyya*, December 20, 2012, para. 10, http://www.jadaliyya.com/pages/index/3643/pioneer-bloggers-in-the-gulf-arab-states.
159. *Ibid.*, 10.
160. "United Arab Emirates: OpenNet Initiative."
161. *Ibid.*

offensive to Muslims and Arabs. The TRA ordered the website and YouTube videos of the "Ahmed and Salim" series blocked in the UAE.[162]

96. The OpenNet initiative's report concluded:

> The UAE continues to prevent its citizens from accessing a significant amount of Internet content spanning a variety of topics. Though the vast majority of sites filtered are those deemed obscene in some way, a select few political sites are blocked, as are some pertaining to Nazis, Holocaust denial and historical revision.[163]

§8. Draft Media Law of 2009 Never Enacted

97. In 2009, the government released a revision to the 1980 Press and Publications Act. Journalists in the UAE were "genuinely excited" with hopes that the new law would provide more protections for journalists and clear up ambiguities surrounding the profession.[164] One writer noted:

> For years the UAE government exercised a fear campaign against journalists, jailing, fining, detaining and interrogating reporters and editors for breaking ambiguous laws. One month, it would be permissible for journalists to report on the sex-trade in the northern emirate of Ra's al-Khaimah; the next they could be summoned for suggesting prostitution is alive and well in the UAE.[165]

98. Some Emirati and expat journalists as well as media watchdog groups report that the legal environment created ambiguity and resulted in self-censorship from the journalists.[166]

99. In many ways, the draft Press Law was a step toward a more-robust journalism in the UAE. The new Media Law, for instance, contained no provisions for jailing journalists. Instead of custodial sentences, the draft Press Law allowed for other sanctions such as fines and/or revocation of a publication's license. The draft law would also give journalists the right to protect confidential sources and mandate that government organizations operate with more transparency and respond to requests for information.[167]

---

162. Dominic von Riedemann, "*UAE Blocks Ahmed and Salim Cartoon*," *Suite 101*, March 4, 2009, http://suite101.com/article/uae-blocks-ahmed-and-salim-cartoon-a100275.
163. "United Arab Emirates: OpenNet Initiative," 38.
164. El-Baltaji, "Emirates Press Law," para. 1.
165. Dana El-Baltaji, "Arab Media & Society," *Arab Media & Society*, Fall 2009, paras. 2–3, http://www.arabmediasociety.com/?article=727.
166. El-Baltaji, "Emirates Press Law"; Andrew Hammond, "*UAE Media Fear Fines, Jail in New Draft Law*," *Reuters*, April 9, 2009, http://www.reuters.com/article/2009/04/13/emirates-media-law-idUSLD4731820090413; "UAE: Media Law Undermines Free Expression," *Human Rights Watch*, April 13, 2009, http://www.hrw.org/news/2009/04/13/uae-media-law-undermines-free-expression.
167. Rahul Sharma, "*Journalists Have Nothing to Fear: Director General, National Media Council*," *Khaleej Times*, February 9, 2009, http://www.khaleejtimes.com/DisplayArticleNew.asp?col=&section=theuae&xfile=data/theuae/2009/February/theuae_February188.xml.

100. However, critics tended to ignore these advances and pointed instead to major drawbacks including huge increases in fines that could actually lead to jail for journalists.[168] Article 32 of the draft Press Law allowed for a fine of up to AED 5 million (USD 1.36 million) for "disparaging" government officials, members of the royal family or Islam. Article 33 would fine journalists up to AED 500,000 (USD 136,000) for "harming the nation's image and reporting 'misleading' information on the economy."[169] These fines were far larger than any penalty in the original Press Law, where fines topped out at AED 20,000 (USD 5,400). Furthermore, failure to pay debts—such as an AED 500,000 fine—in the UAE is a criminal offense and often results in imprisonment. Therefore, the removal of jail for journalists appeared to be only a cosmetic change when the dramatic increase in fines is considered. In effect, the draft Press Law negated the 2007 directive of Sheikh Maktoum bin Rashid, the ruler of Dubai, in which he insisted that journalists should not go to jail as a result of their jobs.

101. Critics of the new Press Law also pointed to the overly broad restrictions such as a prohibition of "disparaging" officials.[170] Journalists reporting on malfeasance in government agencies could easily be accused of disparagement of top officials and face a sizable fine. Such a looming penalty would encourage self-censorship. A report from HRW noted that criticism of public officials was a widely accepted international practice:

102. 'This insulation of public officials from criticism violates the fundamental principle in international human rights law that press freedoms should be wider, not narrower, with respect to speech about politicians and government officials.'[171]

103. Another complaint of the draft Press Law was that it would require an unspecified deposit from media outlets in order for them to operate in the UAE. Under the 1980 Press Law, daily newspapers were required to put an AED 50,000 (USD 13,000) deposit with the government in order to offset any potential penalties. Critics took issue with the unspecified amount in the new law, arguing that the NMC could use the discretion to squeeze out small- and medium-sized media companies.[172]

104. Critics also noted that the law could give the "government power to influence hiring decisions within media organizations."[173] The Press Law also specifically excluded the entities inside the country's free press zones in Dubai, Abu Dhabi, Ra's al-Khaimah, and Fujairah. The demarcation would create a divide between journalists working in the same country on the same stories.[174] Critics included the UAE Journalists Association which submitted a petition signed by 100 journalists asking the government

168. "UAE: Media Law Undermines Free Expression"; El-Baltaji, "Emirates Press Law"; Hammond, "*UAE Media Fear Fines, Jail in New Draft Law.*"
169. El-Baltaji, "Arab Media & Society."
170. "World Report - United Arab Emirates," *Reporters Without Borders*, 2009, http://en.rsf.org/report-united-arab-emirates,150.html; "CPJ Concerned About UAE Draft Media Law," *Committee to Protect Journalists*, March 9, 2009, http://cpj.org/2009/03/cpj-concerned-about-uae-draft-media-law.php.
171. *Just the Good News, Please* (Human Rights Watch, April 6, 2009), 7, http://www.hrw.org/news/2009/04/06/just-good-news-please.
172. "CPJ Concerned About UAE Draft Media Law"; "UAE: Media Law Undermines Free Expression."
173. El-Baltaji, "Arab Media & Society," para. 8.
174. El-Baltaji, "Arab Media & Society."

to consider revising it.[175] The Doha Center for Media Freedom in Qatar also condemned the draft Press Law.[176] While acknowledging that the draft Press Law was a move forward, a report from the advocacy group HRW produced a report with a litany of complaints against it.[177]

105. The NMC issued a point-by-point rebuttal to the HRW report. "Some of the remarks made in the HRW report shows either a real lack of understanding of the situation in the emirates or an attempt to promote concepts and/or procedures that are not compatible with the laws of the UAE and its value system," the NMC said.[178] Najla Al-Awadhi, a member of the FNC, the deliberative body that approved and amended the draft Press Law, reflected the NMC's perspective. She said the revision was a step in the right direction for the country that faced unique circumstances. Al-Awadhi argued that the UAE had to protect itself from tensions provoked by certain press coverage. "We are not trying to emulate the Western ideas of freedom of the press," she said. 'We are a very young country in a very challenging region. We have neighbours that we get along with but also have some tough relationships, like Iran and Pakistan."[179]

106. After much debate and criticism, the draft Press Law was never officially approved and is considered shelved, although it could be signed into law at any time. In 2010, the NMC released a resolution from the chairman directly to media outlets that restated the primacy of the 1980 Media Law (*see* section 3 above.)

§9. Abu Dhabi Media Zone Content Guidelines

107. In 2011, the Abu Dhabi Media Zone Authority (MZA) issued content guidelines that some observers have suggested would work well as a basis for a revised Media Law.[180] The MZA, a media free zone created to encourage media corporation development in the UAE, said the content guidelines were created to balance "freedom of expression with a duty to take account of the social and cultural expectations of society."[181] The code provides guidance on ten specific areas: the protection of children, harm and offense, crime, religion, accuracy and impartiality, fairness, privacy, interactivity, arrangements for funding content (including sponsorship and product placement), and advertising.

---

175. Allia Al Theeb, "Draft Media Law: Journalists 'Will Insist on Changes'," *Gulf News*, April 28, 2009, http://gulfnews.com/news/gulf/uae/media/draft-media-law-journalists-will-insist-on-changes-1.65700.
176. Robin Wigglesworth, "*Rights Group Attacks UAE Draft Media Law*," *Financial Times*, April 13, 2009, http://www.ft.com/cms/s/0/58ccf69c-2817-11de-8dbf-00144feabdc0.html#axzz2SulnXicX.
177. *Just the Good News, Please*.
178. WAM, "UAE National Media Council Welcomes All Debates on Draft Media Law," *Gulf News*, April 13, 2009, para. 8, http://gulfnews.com/news/gulf/uae/media/uae-national-media-council-welcomes-all-debates-on-draft-media-law-1.63826.
179. Hammond, "*UAE Media Fear Fines, Jail in New Draft Law*," para. 17.
180. Matt Duffy, "Revised Media Law for the UAE," accessed January 11, 2013, http://gulfnews.com/opinions/columnists/revised-media-law-for-the-uae-1.998464.
181. *Abu Dhabi Media Zone Content Creation Guidelines* (Abu Dhabi: Media Zone Authority, December 2011), 1, http://twofour54.com/en/media/get/20111026_MZA-CONTENT-CODE-12-October-2011.pdf.

108. The code outlines several areas that journalists should particularly treat with respect: privacy, coverage of the ruling families, and treatment of religion. Respecting these three areas could potentially conflict with critical reporting, but their exclusion from the code seems impossible given the cultural landscape of the UAE. Particularly troublesome is the "respect for ruling families" which could be inferred as overly broad and ambiguous, leading to self-censorship to any media producer operating under the code. The line on where to draw respect for religion is similarly difficult to pinpoint and many countries are still struggling with its boundaries.[182] Most countries generally support protections for privacy with laws that allow for civil damages for invasions of privacy.[183]

109. Rather than simply outlining a long list of prohibitions for media producers—the overwhelming thrust of the 1980 Press and Publications Act as well as the draft Press Law of 2009—the MZA content guidelines offer detailed instruction on the type of journalism that is allowed and tacitly encouraged. The code states that the media is justified in publishing material even if it "has the potential to cause harm" if it meets certain justifications.[184] Under the "fairness" section it lists these editorial justifications:

110. 'The exposure of crime, corruption, antisocial behavior, injustice or serious impropriety, protecting public health or safety, exposing lies, hypocrisy or materially misleading claims made by individuals or organizations, disclosing incompetence, and negligence or dereliction of duty that affects the public.'[185]

111. These justifications represent the type of reports routinely seen in "watchdog" journalism in many countries. These reports—even when they may harm an individual or organization—are explicitly protected either by statutes or court precedents. In many court systems, questions of media behavior that has caused damage (e.g., to reputation) are frequently juxtaposed against the benefit to society provided by robust journalism.[186] This weighing of the benefit of journalism is largely missing in UAE journalism. Reporters, editors, and producers operating under the MZA code as a legal structure would have far more freedom to pursue journalism. If a media regulator, prosecutor, law enforcement official or resident found offense with a report, a judge would have to weigh the charge against these specified editorial justifications.[187] The result would be a far more robust press.[188]

112. It is important to note that the MZA content guidelines do not supersede federal law. The NMC chairman's resolution released quietly to news producers in 2010 (*see* section 3 above) explicitly states that the 1980 Press Law applies to operators inside the media free zones (in Abu Dhabi, Dubai, Ra's al-Khaimah, and Fujairah). A media producer operating within the media free zone of Abu Dhabi would still be held to the legal standards of the Penal Code, 1980 Media Law and 2012 Cybercrime Act.

182. Buckley et al., *Broadcasting, Voice, and Accountability*.
183. Charles Glasser, *International Libel and Privacy Handbook: A Global Reference for Journalists, Publishers, Webmasters, and Lawyers* (John Wiley & Sons, 2010).
184. *MZA Content Code* (Abu Dhabi, UAE: Abu Dhabi Media Zone, 2011),, 14, http://twofour54.com/en/regulatoryaffairs/about-twofour54/mza-licensing.html.
185. *Abu Dhabi Media Zone Content Creation Guidelines*, 14.
186. Tim Crook, *Comparative Media Law and Ethics* (Routledge, 2010).
187. Duffy, "Revised Media Law for the UAE."
188. Of course, this scenario assumes an independent judiciary.

Part II. Regulation of Print, Broadcast, and Digital Media

Chapter 1. The Journalists' Profession

§1. Notion and Regulation

113. Journalists are heavily regulated in the UAE through the Media Law and other restrictive legal and cultural provisions. The notion of journalism, therefore, is limited to restrained criticism and furthering the goals of the government. Few reporters and editors engage in the type of journalism, for instance, espoused by Kovach and Rosenthiel in their book "Principles of Journalism." These nine principles include commitments to truth and verification, independence from powerful figures and institutions, space for public criticism and compromise, loyalty to citizens, and comprehensive and proportional reporting. The principles also stress the need for an impartial method of reporting that values verification instead of assertion to create "a reliable version of events."[189]

114. In his book "Arab Mass Media," Rugh coined the term "loyalist press" for the journalism profession in the UAE and several other Arab countries. "The loyalist press tends to be more passive," he writes. "On the whole, it avoids some critical issues, it is slower to react editorially to events, and it tends to be more muted in its commentaries."[190] Journalists generally "avoid the language and opinions of revolutionary journalism which are the characteristic of the mobilization press, in which continuously do battle with enemies and evils, real or imagined … ."[191] Perhaps much of the reason for a press that behaves in a loyalist fashion can be traced back in part to the diligent regulation of journalists and the relative lack of legal protections for their work. The following section outlines the regulations for journalists working in the UAE.

115. The 1980 Press and Publications Act mandates rules for newspaper ownership and the registration of journalists. The law also allows for the withdrawal of credentials and refers to deportation of journalists who violate various prohibitions (*see* Article 28, No.5.)

189. Bill Kovach and Tom Rosenstiel, *The Elements of Journalism: What Newspeople Should Know and The Public Should Expect* (Three Rivers Press, 2007), 77.
190. Rugh, *Arab Mass Media*, 66.
191. *Ibid.*

116. Chapter 4 of the 1980 Press Law pertains to newspapers, periodicals, and news agencies and Article 24 mandates that no newspaper shall be published without receiving the permissions demanded in the law. The NMC chairman's resolution of 2010 stated that the law applied to all "visible, audible and legible" media in the country (*see* Part I, section 3 for more).[192] Therefore, all discussion in this chapter will refer to all news media instead of solely newspapers as explicitly written in the 1980 law.

117. Article 25 requires that the owner of media outlets must:

(1) Be a UAE national. This requirement is waived for diplomatic missions and foreign news agencies licensed to operate in the UAE.
(2) Shall not be less than 25 years old.
(3) Shall be "fully competent."
(4) Shall be of good conduct and behavior.
(5) Shall not have been convicted of an offence involving "moral turpitude" or had their moral standing restored by the "proper authority" following a conviction.
(6) Shall not occupy public service post in country.
(7) Shall not be employed by foreign agency in country.

118. Article 26 mandates that the media outlet must have an "editor-in-chief" who supervises its content. Conversely, media outlets may have a number of editors who each hold responsibility for specific sections of the media outlet. The owner may be the editor-in-chief or he may employment a "responsible editor" who meets the legal requirements.

119. Article 27 mandates that an editor-in-chief shall have a higher degree from a recognized university or other institute of learning. He should also have "full experience" to perform his job.

120. Article 28 also provides basic requirements for writers or editors at the media outlets. These requirements are similar to the previous criteria for editor-in-chief. The article also mandates that writers and editors either have a degree from a higher education institute or at least three years of experience as a journalist. An official with the NMC said that this requirement was not enforced in practice.[193]

121. The article also prohibits the employment of any journalist who had previously "been ordered to leave the country for an offense related to publishing."[194] That directive indicates that asking foreigners to leave the country for various offences is fairly commonplace. The article also exempts UAE nationals from the requirement related to education and experience.

122. Article 29 mandates that all editors and writers register with the government before they start work. Their nationality and place of residence must be registered as well. The NMC, formed in 2006, handles journalism registration for the now-defunct Ministry of Information and Culture mentioned in the 1980 law.

123. Article 30 mandates the foreign correspondents for outside publications must register with the ministry. A NMC official noted that this article is not enforced

192. *Resolution of the Chairman Regarding the Media Content Criterion* (Abu Dhabi, UAE: National Media Council, 2010), http://www.scribd.com/doc/111698636.
193. Hellyer, Personal Communication.
194. *UAE: 1980 Press and Publications Act.*

in practice. While some foreign journalists do register with the NMC—and receive a press card—many others operate in the country without notifying their agency.[195]

124. Article 31 mandates that anyone wishing to publish a newspaper or launch a news outlet must register with the ministry and include basic information on the editors including nationality, place of residence, and professional qualifications.

125. Article 32 prescribes that the ministry must support the application of a news outlet. Then, the federal cabinet (the ministers of various federal ministries) must approve the application.

126. Articles 34 and 35 of the law mandate a deposit of AED 50,000 (USD 13,500) for daily newspaper and AED 25,000 (USD 6,750) for all other media outlets to be paid to the ministry. The deposit ensures "settlement of fines imposed by the provisions of this law or any other law."[196] These deposits must be maintained at appropriate levels as fines are processed.

127. Article 36 holds that the media outlet cannot publish or broadcast if their license expires or if ordered to shut down by any proper authority.

128. Article 37 requires the name of the editors and other identifying information be included on every issue on either the front or last page of the publication.

129. Article 38 mandates that five copies of newspapers be dropped off at the ministry upon publication. Same-day updates of issues must also be delivered to the ministry. Obviously, these directives are difficult to apply to the other news media.

130. Article 39 requires the publishing of any notice sent by federal ministries free of charge. These notices must be published "in places where important news is published."[197]

131. The rest of the law provides layers of regulations around other forms of media. Articles 49 through 53 regulate the importation of news products and books into the UAE. Articles 54 through 69 concern the importation and censorship of films.

132. These regulations contribute to a severely restricted legal environment for journalists, contributing to the preponderance of a "loyalist press."[198] In countries with more robust press freedoms, the governments do not license journalists or media outlets.[199] Some courts have ruled that licensing journalists would create undue pressure on the profession that may lead to self-censorship when covering issues related to government officials.[200]

§2. Subsidies to the Press

133. The government—or members of the ruling families who act in concert with the government—subsidizes or owns much of the media in the UAE. However, because of the general lack of transparency with government accounting, the exact

195. Hellyer, Personal Communication.
196. *UAE: 1980 Press and Publications Act.*
197. *Ibid.*
198. Rugh, *Arab Mass Media.*
199. Buckley et al., *Broadcasting, Voice, and Accountability.*
200. "Licensing of Media Workers," *Article 19*, accessed March 25, 2013, http://www.article19.org/pages/en/licensing-of-media-workers.html.

numbers of these subsidies are impossible to determine. Even the ownership of each press outlet can prove difficult to pin down with certainty. At least one "private" newspaper features 30% minority ownership from the Dubai government. Also, members of the royal family have ownership in some "private" newspapers, so the distinction between government-owned and private becomes murky at best.[201]

134. Some media observers report that "private media do not exist in the true sense in the UAE."[202] They note that privately owned outlets receive support from the government in the form of large advertising contracts. This support, they say, leads to self-censorship and a disincentive to criticize government offices.[203]

201. Rugh, *Arab Mass Media*.
202. *UAE: Media Sustainability Index*, 198.
203. *UAE: Media Sustainability Index*.

Chapter 2. Journalists' Rights

§1. No Role of Journalists as Watchdogs of Society

135. The "watchdog" role of the press is generally not recognized in the UAE, the Gulf states, and generally in the Arab region. As Ruff said, "The concept of the watchdog function of the media acting for the public against the government is manifest only in limited ways in the Arab world."[204] The local press addresses the issue from time to time. In 2010, the Abu Dhabi editor of Gulf News noted that "journalists are no longer doing their duty, meaning that the press is no longer monitoring the performance of government."[205] Instead, the press tends to tone down coverage so that government officials are not angered. An Emirati professor at UAE University, Dr. Abdulla Abdulkhaleq, said that the government used its regulatory powers to cower the press. The government "has done everything possible to gently court the media, keep it happy but under its tight benevolent watch. The government has made sure that the media does not develop an independent mind of its own."[206]

136. Observers argue that the result of overbearing government actions and a weak legal structure is a culture in which "watchdog" journalism is not appreciated, rewarded, or allowed to grow.[207]

137. Furthermore, the "rights" of a journalist is essentially an unknown concept in the UAE. In addition to a weak legal standing, almost all the journalists in the UAE are expatriates (estimates suggest more than 90%). Out of fear of deportation, many journalists learn the location of the "red lines" in coverage. These unofficial boundaries include any criticism of the royal family, discussion of certain cultural subjects, coverage of the security services, and reporting that reflects poorly on the business environment. The expatriate journalists and their Emirati peers avoid any critical journalism that could violate these unwritten rules.[208] As a result of this environment, the journalism profession is treated as no more important for society than any other layman's job. The practice of corruption and lack of strong ethical standards among UAE journalists may be linked to this general lack of respect for the journalism profession.

138. The Qatar Peninsula, a newspaper in a nearby Gulf country, described in 2011 the fate of journalists in its country. In a scathingly honest front-page editorial titled "The Crippled Fourth Estate,"[209] two writers for the paper explained how the press functioned in the country. Two Emirati commentators noted on social media the

---

204. Rugh, *Arab Mass Media*, 16.
205. Rasheed, "*The Ceiling of Press Freedom in UAE Is Falling*," 3.
206. Abdulkhaleq, "*Ups and Downs of UAE Rankings*," paras 8–9.
207. El-Baltaji, "Emirates Press Law"; Rasheed, "*The Ceiling of Press Freedom in UAE Is Falling.*"
208. Rugh, *Arab Mass Media*.
209. "The Fourth Estate" is a term commonly used to refer to the news media. Political theorist Edmund Burke coined the usage in 1787 during a debate to open the British House of Commons to journalists.

situation described in the paper applied to the news outlets in the UAE and other Gulf countries.[210] The newspaper detailed:

> Reporters are viewed as an easy prey by those who disapprove of or are offended by their writings. In countries which have media freedom and extensive laws to protect the media, defamation suits are filed against reporters and their newspapers directly by those aggrieved. In Qatar, however, the situation is different in the absence of a media law. Here, anybody can simply file a complaint with the police against a reporter and his newspaper. The police then call the reporter and question him in a harassing way, and if they (the police) feel there is merit in the complaint, the journalist is referred to the Public Prosecution for further questioning.
>
> Since it is the prosecution's prerogative to refer a matter to court, many complaints against journalists do not reach the court at all and end up in journalists being harassed and humiliated rather than being put on a fair trial. Many a time prosecution officials call a journalist concerned at 5am, when he is in the middle of sleep. The entire process is so harrowing and humiliating for a journalist that he chickens out when it comes to writing critically on issues. Since most journalists in Qatar are foreigners, they obviously want to stay clear of trouble, say media sources. "No one would, obviously, want to be treated like a criminal for writing critically", says a journalist who was once called by the police for questioning in a defamation-related complaint. And even if a journalist shows guts and is willing to do critical or informative writing, he has no access to officials to get basic information.[211]

139. In addition to the easy harassment of journalists, the authors also blamed the weak legal protections for journalists, self-censorship from managing editors who favor job security over good journalism, and the news media's tangled web of loyalties to big businesses and the government. The UAE shares these traits leaving journalists to largely operate at the whim of the government officials in charge.[212] The press in the UAE, therefore, does not truly function as a critical check on powerful institutions but rather as an organ of the state.[213] In effect, the type of criticism that *is* raised in UAE papers has already been given approval. The "red lines" in coverage are well-established.[214]

---

210. Matt Duffy, "Peninsula Journalism Attack Resonates Regionally," *Mideast Posts*, June 6, 2011, http://mideastposts.com/2011/03/peninsula-attack-on-journalism-rings-true-region-wide/.
211. "A Crippled Fourth Estate," paras. 20–28, accessed January 10, 2013, http://thepeninsulaqatar.com//144697-.html.
212. Duffy, "Peninsula Journalism Attack Resonates Regionally."
213. Rasheed, "*The Ceiling of Press Freedom in UAE Is Falling.*"
214. El-Baltaji, "Emirates Press Law."

§2. Limited Protections for Journalists

140. As previously detailed, the UAE Constitution contains no provision specifically protecting the press. And the Media Law outlines a series of prohibitions for journalists but virtually no wording that defines or defends their role in the society. Journalists do enjoy a ban on imprisonment for offenses as well as access to court proceedings. They also receive limited protection for public discussion as well as statutory right to the "fair use" of copyrighted material. These protections will be detailed below.

I. No Jail for Journalists

141. In 2007, Sheikh Maktoum bin Rashid, the ruler of Dubai and prime minister of the UAE, issued instructions "that journalists in the country will not be jailed for doing their work."[215] He made the statement two days after two journalists—Indian and Egyptian expatriates—had been sentenced to two months in jail after losing a libel case. Shortly after the announcement, the journalists for the English-language newspaper Khaleej Times were released by an appeals court decree.[216] The announcement came from the head of the NMC, Sheikh Abdullah bin Zayed al-Nahayan, a member of the royal family in Abu Dhabi. Sheikh Mohammad did note that "other measures can be taken to penalize a journalist who has committed a particular violation."[217] Sheikh Abdullah, the NMC chief, announced that the ruler of Dubai had also asked for UAE Cabinet, the heads of the federal government ministries, to approve changes to the 1980 Media Law after consulting with the NMC and other parties.

142. The local press enthusiastically welcomed Sheikh Maktoum's statement against the jailing of journalists. Dubai's Gulf News declared in a large headline on the front-page: "UAE upholds press freedom."[218] The UAE Journalists Association praised the decision. Mohammad Yousuf, chairman of the association, said the move "reflects the leadership's support for the press and journalists, and its backing for freedom of speech and the right of expression."[219] While a revision of the Press Law was released in 2009, it was never enacted. One of the main complaints was that the draft Press Law did not provide enough protection and too many restrictions for journalists. (*See* Part I, section 8 for more details.) In 2010, the Emirates News Agency indicated that since the declaration banning the jailing of journalists came from a member of the Federal Supreme Council, the law should be considered officially changed. "All that is left is to amend the law to conform with the order, which is a

215. Samir, "*UAE Upholds Press Freedom.*"
216. The timing of the appeals court release—immediately following the sheikh's statement—points to the lack of judicial independence in the country.
217. . https://eng-archive.aawsat.com/theaawsat/media-news/uae-rules-journalists-not-to-be-jailed-over-work.
218. Salama Samir, "*UAE Upholds Press Freedom,*" *Gulf News*, September 25, 2007, http://gulfnews.com/news/gulf/uae/media/uae-upholds-press-freedom-1.202309.
219. *Ibid.*, para. 7.

matter of time and procedure," according to the official news agency.[220] As of 2016, the law concerning jail for journalists has not yet been officially updated.

II. Access to Trials

143. Article 47 of the 1980 Press and Publications Law grants journalists access to trials. The article says journalists may "quote arguments and pleadings" in the courts. The law also allows a judge to bar journalists from attending if the hearing is closed. Access to public trials is a well-established right in countries with developed media freedoms. Court precedents in other countries often favor journalists, holding that trials publicized by the media benefit from the transparency.[221]

144. However, Article 265 of the Penal Code prohibits inaccurate reporting from an open court. It states: "Shall also be liable to the same hereinabove specified punishment any individual who, with his honesty and in bad faith publishes, through any means of publicity, what has taken place during the hearings in open court."[222] Statutes that prohibit erroneous journalism (except in cases of defamation) tend to hamper independent reporting since a government official and a journalist might not agree about what constitutes truth and error. (*See* Chapter 3, Journalist's Liability, section 5, for more on "false news.")

III. Weak Protection for Public Discussion

145. The only other protection for journalists in the UAE law is a provision in Article 46 of the 1980 Media Law. The article states "newspapers may publish articles that discuss political, economic, scientific, or literary issues, or other issues of public interest unless publications of such issues are prohibited."[223] The provision implies that the role of the press is to provide a space for open dialogue and discussion of issues. But, Article 98 of the same law makes broad prohibitions on publishing materials that could cause harm to the country, damage unity and federation, or threaten public order. The prohibitions of Article 98 effectively undercut the guarantees of Article 46. Many discussions of political or economic interests could be perceived to cause harm to the country and damage unity. The wording could result in a press that steers away from many economic and political issues despite receiving specific legal allowance to cover those topics.

220. *Journalists and Writers Associations Slam HRW Report*, para. 9.
221. Buckley et al., *Broadcasting, Voice, and Accountability*.
222. *United Arab Emirates Penal Code, Federal Law*, 1987, http://www.scribd.com/doc/122309224/UAE-Penal-Code-amended-1987.
223. *UAE: 1980 Press and Publications Act*.

IV. Fair Use

146. Article 46 of the UAE Press and Publications Act specifically allows for the use of short quotations from other works, essentially creating a boundary for the copyright concept of "fair use." The law bans wholesale copying of complete works but allows for a quotation or "brief notes" without consent of the author. Article 23 of the UAE Copyright Law of 1992 also provides for "fair use" protections for newspapers and other publications.[224] The concept of fair use is internationally recognized as a middle ground between openly violating the copyrights of authors and completely prohibiting the any reproduction of works. Courts and legal systems have reasoned that the latter would squelch free and open discussion of issues, leading to societal harm.[225]

§3. No Protection of Journalistic Sources

147. Journalists in the UAE receive no legal protection to keep their sources confidential. Guarantees that journalists can keep their sources of information secret often help the press perform their function as a watchdog on corporate and government dealings. Journalists must often promise anonymity to sources providing information about sensitive subjects, out of fear of reprisals by people in positions of power. If sources cannot be assured that journalists will not be compelled to reveal their sources, then these channels of information may dry up. Such a development would hamper the free flow of information and hurt the public interest. Several countries guarantee confidentiality between journalists and their sources either through the Constitution (e.g., Argentina), statutes (e.g., the individual states in the United States), or legal precedent (e.g., Nigeria and Bermuda).[226] The UAE's draft Press Law of 2009 contained some provisions for allowing journalists to protect their sources. The draft was never signed into law after a several other complaints about its other provisions.

§4. Lack of Transparency, Access to Information

148. A common complaint for journalists is the general lack of transparency in dealings with governments and businesses—both in the UAE and across the Gulf states. An Emirati columnist discussed the issue in a 2011 editorial in Dubai's Gulf News. Mishaal al Gergawi referred to the lack of government representatives who would speak to the press and hamstrung media in the Gulf countries. (To bypass the stifled media system, columnists often refer to problems with "Gulf governments," when the criticism is actually directed toward UAE officials.) Al Gergawi noted "every time I read an article relating to the recent political developments in the Gulf I look

224. Brian Fitzgerald and Rami Olwan, "Copyright Law in the United Arab Emirates in the Digital Age," *European Intellectual Property Review* 32, no. 11 (2010): 565–574.
225. Gillian Davies, *Copyright and the Public Interest*, 2nd ed. (Sweet & Maxwell, 2002).
226. Buckley et al., *Broadcasting, Voice, and Accountability*.

for a government statement but rarely find one."[227] He suggested that governments give spokespeople the information they need and empower them to communicate it to journalists and the public. Al Gergawi also made a call to "liberate the local media," allowing it to cover issues with the same vigor as the external press.[228] Government officials often withhold basic information from journalists and refuse to answer their questions, perhaps a reflection of the general lack of respect for the profession.

149. Journalists are granted little access to information regarding the country's spending. No law upholds any rights to access of information from the media or residents. The draft Press Law of 2009 did contain a provision that ordered government entities to ease the flow of information to the media. However, the Press Law was never enacted after widespread criticism of its other provisions. As one report put it, UAE "journalists must rely on their personal connections to obtain the information they need."[229]

227. Al Gergawi, "*Incommunicado*," para. 1.

228. *Ibid*., para. 15.

229. *Oman Media Sustainability Index* (Washington, D.C.: IREX, 2009), 199, http://www.irex.org/resource/oman-media-sustainability-index-msi.

Chapter 3. Journalists' Liability

§1. Defamation and Libel

150. Before discussing defamation law in the UAE, it will be helpful to understand the approach taken in countries that embrace the ICCPR model balancing freedom of expression with legitimate curbs on speech and the press (*see* section 1, Part I above.) In many countries, public officials and business leaders use defamation laws to silence unwanted criticism. The journalistic duty to expose corruption and hold government and businesses to account can be severely hampered by defamation laws that allow people and institutions to protect reputations that they do not deserve.[230]

151. The international approach toward defamation in countries with strong protections for press freedom generally requires three elements to allow for penalties against journalists. The news report must:

(1) Be false.
(2) Be disseminated to an audience.
(3) Cause damage to reputation.[231]

152. In addition to these three criteria, defamed parties must also show that the journalists were negligent in their duties (i.e., did not follow proper journalistic procedures to verify the information).[232] Furthermore, many countries also require an even greater level of negligence (i.e., knowingly disregarded the truth) if the report focuses on a public figure.[233] International law generally holds that public officials require less defamation protection because their position provides more opportunity for criticism from the public.[234]

153. One generally held principle in countries that embrace the ICCPR framework is that defamation cases are heard as civil matters rather than criminal complaints.[235] In these countries, journalists or media outlets that lose libel lawsuits pay the defamed parties compensatory and punitive damages but do not face prison sentences or other criminal penalties. This general approach toward defamation is seen throughout the world (not just in "Western" countries) in localities as diverse as Chile, Japan, South Korea, Costa Rica, the European Union, Canada, and the United States.[236] In several

230. Buckley et al., *Broadcasting, Voice, and Accountability*.
231. Glasser, *International Libel and Privacy Handbook*.
232. *Civil Defamation: Undermining Free Expression* (London: Article 19, 2009), http://www.article19.org/resources.php/resource/1427/en/civil-defamation.
233. W. Wat Hopkins, ed., *Communication and the Law 2012* (Vision Press, 2012).
234. Buckley et al., *Broadcasting, Voice, and Accountability*.
235. Peter N. 1961- Amponsah, *Libel Law, Political Criticism, and Defamation of Public Figures: the United States, Europe, and Australia /*, Law and Society (New York, N.Y.) (LFB Scholarly Pub., 2004).
236. Glasser, *International Libel and Privacy Handbook*.

countries—Bosnia-Herzegovina (2002), Central African Republic (2004), Georgia (2004), Ghana (2001), Sri Lanka (2002), Togo (2004), and Ukraine (2001)—criminal defamation laws have recently been eliminated completely.[237] In these countries and many others, the civil courts have been found to be an adequate remedy to protect reputation. The African Court of Human and Peoples' Rights ruled in 2014 that criminal defamation in Burkina Faso violated freedom of expression.[238] The court joined similar rulings from the Inter-American Court of Human Rights and the European Court of Human Rights.[239]

154. Another principle embraced by countries that follow the ICCPR model is the concept that truth is an ultimate defense for defamation. In these countries, journalists cannot lose a libel case if they simply reported the truth.[240] This approach ensures that no one can defend a good reputation that they do not in reality deserve. The European Court of Human Rights ruled that a writer had his right to free expression violated because Spain did not allow him the opportunity to prove the truth of his statements in a defamation case.[241] The case created a precedent across Europe of truth as a defense for defamation. The Declaration of Principles on Freedom of Expression in Africa, passed in 2002, suggested that all African countries include truth as a defense for libel as part of their legal systems.[242]

155. The result of these international approaches toward defamation is an environment that forces the press to operate responsibly but offers protection so that powerful people and institutions cannot squelch independent reporting with easy-to-win defamation charges.

156. The UAE's approach toward defamation creates a restrictive environment for journalists. Defamation cases are handled as criminal rather than civil matters under legislation from the Penal Code and the Press and Publications Act. Plaintiffs may sue for defamation to collect civil claims, but they do so under general principles of tort (i.e., "wrongful acts causing harm").[243] In criminal defamation cases, the state brings action against a party accused of defamation with a guilty verdict leading to a fine or jail time. As mentioned above, this approach differs with the approach in jurisdictions with freer media systems where libel (written defamation) and slander (spoken defamation) are handled as a civil case between two parties that could result in a monetary judgment, but not criminal penalties such as jail time or fines.[244]

157. The criminal nature of defamation laws in the UAE means that speakers and journalists can never be sure when their words may lead to trouble since even

237. Buckley et al., *Broadcasting, Voice, and Accountability.*

238. http://mediadefence.org/news/african-court-delivers-landmark-ruling-criminal-libel.

239. https://www.ifex.org/costa_rica/2004/08/06/inter_american_court_of_human_rights/; https://www.article19.org/resources.php/resource/2586/en/lingens-v.-austria.

240. *Ibid.*

241. *Castells v. Spain* (Strasbourg, France: European Court of Human Rights, April 23, 1992), http://www.elaw.org/node/5580.

242. "Declaration of Principles on Freedom of Expression in Africa," 2002, sec. 12, http://www1.umn.edu/humanrts/achpr/expressionfreedomdec.html.

243. Rebecca Kelly & Sharon Procter, *Defamation and Social Media in the UAE* (Dubai, UAE: Clyde & Co, September 25, 2012), http://www.clydeco.com/insight/updates/defamation-and-social-media-in-the-uae.

244. Buckley et al., *Broadcasting, Voice, and Accountability.*

truthful and verified reporting could result in an arrest. One journalist who examined the criminal defamation laws as a reporter for The National in Abu Dhabi, said that the laws contributed to a culture of self-censorship in the UAE. "The defamation laws add to the belief that the system is set against you as a journalist," said Kevin Brass, who worked as a business reporter for The National from 2011–2012. "Even if you are in the right, by conventional journalistic standards, there can be serious consequences if an accusation is made against you. And the legal structure will not necessarily support you."[245] Reporters or editors occasionally ignore or drastically alter the coverage of a story out of worry that their reporting could lead to a criminal defamation charge.[246]

158. The laws on defamation can be found in various sections of the Penal Code, the Press and Publications Law, parts of the Constitution, and other federal legislation.

159. The articles in section 6 of the Penal Code of 1987 contain provisions that criminalize acts that harm reputations or reveal secrets. The law aims to protect an individual's honor as well as his private life. (For more on privacy legislation, *see* section 2 below.)

160. In its statutory definition of defamation, Article 372 of the Penal Code makes it a crime when a "person attributes to others through any public means an instance that may subject the person to punishment and contempt." The penalty for defamation is imprisonment for up to two years and a fine of AED 20,000 (USD 5,400). The law dictates certain circumstances that will be considered aggravating factors during sentencing. Aggravating circumstances include defamation against a civil servant of someone providing a public service or the publication of the defamation in a newspaper or other printed media. Legal observers consider social media such as Facebook and Twitter as "printed media" because of their ability to reach a wide audience.[247]

161. Article 373 holds that statements harming the "honor" of another person would also be punishable. The exact delineation between provoking "contempt" (Article 372) and harming a person's "honor" (Article 373) is unclear and apparently up to the discretion of prosecutors. Article 373 provides less punishment than its predecessor—just one year in prison or a AED 10,000 fine (USD 2,700). The aforementioned aggravating circumstances applying to public officials also apply.

162. As mentioned earlier, creating a special layer of defamatory protection for public officials differs with the approach of countries with greater journalism protections and other rulings from human rights courts. In many countries public officials find it harder to win defamation cases because the nature of their jobs invites more criticism.

163. Article 374 of the law states that defamation can occur via telephone or in person and carries a fine of up to AED 5,000 (USD 1,350). The law stipulates an extra six months for making the defamatory statement in front of others. In this sense, the defamation law appears more closely aligned with a prohibition against insults since most legal jurisdictions define defamation as a statement made to a wider audience.

164. Article 375 concerns an important element of libel law, whether the truth of the statement can be used as a defense for defamation. In many countries, truth is

245. Kevin Brass, Personal Communication, Email, April 30, 2013.
246. Matt Duffy, "Civil Courts Should Handle Defamation," *Gulf News*, November 18, 2011, http://gulfnews.com/opinions/columnists/civil-courts-should-handle-defamation-1.932729.
247. Kelly and Procter, *Defamation and Social Media in the UAE*.

an ultimate defense for libel. By drawing this distinction for true statements, reports that are true, yet embarrassing, cannot be deemed as libelous and punish the speaker. Article 375 states that:

> there is no crime if the offender proves the reality of the incident which he imputed to the victim, whenever such incrimination is performed against a public officer or a person to whom a public service is assigned and whenever the said incident is connected with the function or service.

165. Legal observers agree that the wording of this statute makes it difficult to understand its exact meaning.[248] The article appears to provide truth as a defense, but only if the figure allegedly defamed is a public official or carrying out a public act. However, the act could also be read to mean that truth is a defense in all cases. The result is an unclear perception of the exact meaning of law that leaves observers unsure of the exact parameters. One lawyer said truth is not an "absolute" defense in the UAE.[249] This lack of clear distinction regarding truth as a defense for libel creates a palpable disadvantage for journalists in the UAE.

166. Article 375 also states that the burden of proof in a defamation case rests on the defendant and contains a statute of limitations of five years on any defamatory statement.

167. Article 376 protects defamatory statements made in court proceedings. Article 377 offers a privilege for individuals who make a "a defamatory statement in the context of assisting official authorities or with a good intention."[250] The article appears aimed to protecting individuals who report a crime to authorities.

168. The next three articles involve privacy rights. Article 378 prohibits eavesdropping unless the victim gives consent. Article 379 makes it illegal to distribute a secret for private benefit. Article 380 makes it illegal to eavesdrop on a conversation or open someone's mail. Penalties range from AED 1,000 (270 USD) to AED 20,000 (5,400 USD) and some jail time.

169. The 1980 Press and Publications Law contains other provisions surrounding defamation charges and the news media.

170. Article 100 of the Press Law states that reports of defamation should be made to a judicial officer who would then choose whether to bring action. This procedure follows the rights under Article 41 of the UAE Constitution to "submit complaints to the competent authorities, including the judicial authorities, concerning the abuse or infringement of the rights and freedom stipulated in this Part Three."[251]

171. Article 77 provides a blanket prohibition of defamation that applies to "Arabs and their civilization." The article makes no mention of truth as a defense for the defamation, so reporting on any Arab that injures his or her reputations could conceivably be a violation of law. Article 84 offers specific protection for defamation of public officials. The article reads: "It is prohibited to malign a public official, or anybody occupying a post in the public prosecution, or assigned to perform a public

248. Rizvi, *Personal Communication.*
249. Brass, '*Defamation Laws Keep the Aggrieved Quiet.*'
250. Mullis, *Carter-Ruck on Libel and Slander.*
251. *Ibid.*

job. The writer shall not be held responsible if he proves he did so in good faith." The final sentence provides some protection for a journalist if he or she can show just cause for highlighting the information that caused the public figure's defamation. However, the article creates more protection for public officials rather than the international standard that generally forces public officials to tolerate more criticism than their private peers.

172. The updated Cybercrime Law of 2012 appears to contain the most restrictive provision regarding defamation in the UAE. Article 20 allows for both a large fine and imprisonment for anyone who "accuses another person of a matter of which he shall be subject to punishment or being held in contempt by others by using a computer network or an information technology means."[252] This description meets the statutory definition of defamation. The article contains no provision for using truth as a defense, so reporting or discussing factual statements in an electronic setting could result in a violation of the law. Furthermore, the law considers a "slander ... against a public official or service in the course of or because of his work" an aggravating factor of the crime. Again, the law allows for more protection for public figures rather than less. The penalties are far harsher than the Penal Code allows for defamation—at least AED 250,000 (USD 67,500) and up to AED 500,000 (USD 135,000). In comparison, the maximum fine for defamation in the Penal Code is AED 20,000 (USD 5,400). In addition, Article 20 allows for "imprisonment" but offers no guidance on the minimum or maximum terms unlike most of the other articles in the law.

173. The Dubai Court of Cassation has upheld charges of defamation for statements that resulted in "punishment" or "humiliation" in their community. The court also held that "mere criticism" may also be regarded as defamatory if the statement exceeds the "normal limits" or affects the honor of the person defamed.[253] It is important to note that Dubai's court system is officially separate from the other emirates and that precedent in previous cases rarely guides court rulings in the UAE. (*See* section 10, "Case Studies," below for specific examples of defamation cases.)

§2. Privacy

174. Laws to protect privacy can be found in the nation's Constitution, the federal Penal Code, the Press and Publications Law of 1980, and the Cybercrime Law of 2012. The right to privacy is a well-established international standard. Article 8 of the European Convention on Human Rights, for instance, states that "Everyone has the right to respect for his private and family life, his home and his correspondence."[254] The declaration notes that some exceptions "in accordance with law" can be carried out for "the interests of national security, public safety or the economic well-being of the country, for the prevention of disorder or crime, for the protection of health or morals, or for the protection of the rights and freedoms of others."[255]

252. *UAE Cybercrime Law of 2012.*
253. Kelly and Procter, *Defamation and Social Media in the UAE.*
254. *Council of Europe: Convention for the Protection of Human Rights and Fundamental Freedoms*, 2010, http://conventions.coe.int/treaty/en/Treaties/Html/005.htm.
255. *Ibid.*

175. Article 31 of the UAE Constitution states: "Freedom of communication by post, telegraph or other means of communication and the secrecy thereof shall be guaranteed in accordance with law." The Constitution therefore protects the secrecy of a wide variety of communication and several legal provisions guarantee that protection.

176. Article 378 of the Penal Code creates a criminal penalty against the disclosure of confidential information. The method of disclosure is unstated, so the law could apply to a wide variety of circumstances. The article specifically mentions photographs as type of confidential information, leading many legal advisors in the UAE to suggest caution when taking and sharing pictures. The confidential information need not be defamatory or erroneous, only that its "secrets of private or family lives of individuals."[256] Penalties for violations can result in up to one year in jail or a fine of AED 10,000 (USD 2,700).

177. Article 379 of the Penal Code provides penalties when an official discloses private information of a third party that was gained while the individual was working in a "profession, craft or art."[257] Article 380 of the Penal Code prohibits interception of communication between others. While the article specifically refers to letters and telegrams as well as eavesdropping on a phone call, one legal text notes that the "provision is likely to have a wider application to cover new forms of communications media."[258] Violators face a fine of AED 3,000 (USD 800). The fine rises to AED 5,000 (USD 1,350) and a three-month jail term if the intercepted communication is communicated to a third party. The increased penalty could obviously apply to journalists who illegally gain and share private information.

178. The 1980 Press and Publications Act contains several provisions forbidding divulging information from private lives. Article 79 states: "No news, pictures, comments about an individuals' private life shall be published if their publication is meant to disgrace such individuals."[259] The act goes on to forbid the disclosure of any secret that may affect a person's reputation, wealth or trade name. The press is also banned from divulging information if the intention is coercion or blackmail.

179. Article 8 of the Cybercrime Law also contains privacy provisions. Article 21 provides punishment for the following three ways in which a person's privacy may be invaded:

(1) Eavesdropping, interception, recording, transferring, transmitting or disclosure of conversations or communications, or audio or visual materials.
(2) Photographing others or creating, transferring, disclosing, copying or saving electronic photos.
(3) Publishing news, electronic photos or photographs, scenes, comments, statements, or information even if true and correct.[260]

256. Mullis, *Carter-Ruck on Libel and Slander*.
257. Simon Adams & Sara Khoja, *Confidentiality and Your Business in the Middle East* (Clyde & Co, July 22, 2010), http://www.mondaq.com/x/106066/employee+rights+labour+relations/Confidentiality+and+your+business+in+the+Middle+East.
258. Mullis, *Carter-Ruck on Libel and Slander*.
259. *UAE: 1980 Press and Publications Act*.
260. *UAE Cybercrime Law of 2012*.

180. Punishments can include at least six months imprisonment and a fine of between AED 150,000 and AED 500,000 (USD 40,500 and USD 135,000). The last provision regarding "publishing news" would apply to both journalists in the UAE as well as anyone using social media sites to document any type of public event.

181. Article 22 increases the Penal Code penalty for releasing confidential information dramatically. While the Penal Code provides for a fine of AED 10,000 (USD 2,700), the Cybercrime Law allows for a fine of up to AED 1,000,000 (USD 270,000) for disclosing "confidential information which he has obtained in the course of or because of his work" via an electronic resource.

182. As stated above, the right to privacy is an internationally recognized right. Generally, international courts will side with individuals in cases concerning invasions of privacy unless an overwhelming public benefit can be found in disclosure of private information. However, care is taken to ensure that privacy laws do not affect the free flow of information that would benefit the public.[261]

§3. Public Order and National Security

183. The restriction of media and other forms of expression to protect "public order" and "national security" is an internationally recognized legal precedent. For instance, Article 19 of the United Nations' ICCPR guarantees freedom of expression but restricts such rights in certain specific circumstances including "for the protection of national security or of public order."[262] Public order tends to refer to disruptions of harmonious living among the residents of the country. National security can refer both to the stability of public order or as a threat from outside the county to destabilize the government. The question of how to best balance public order and national security restrictions without stifling freedom of expression is determined by individual nations.[263]

184. Some nations have approached the need for such restrictions with caution so as not to infringe on healthy public dialogue. If any speech critical of the government is deemed a danger to public order, then the effect on free and open discussion can be quite chilling. The 1995 "Johannesburg Principles: National Security, Freedom of Expression and Access to Information" outlined an ideal course of action for governments to take while weighing freedom of expression with the need to protect national security. The guidelines aimed to:

> promote a clear recognition of the limited scope of restrictions on freedom of expression and freedom of information that may be imposed in the interest of national security, so as to discourage governments from using the pretext of national security to place unjustified restrictions on the exercise of these freedoms.[264]

---

261. "Declaration of Principles on Freedom of Expression in Africa."
262. *International Covenant on Civil and Political Rights.*
263. The UAE is not a signatory to the Covenant.
264. *The Johannesburg Principles on National Security, Freedom of Expression and Access to Information* (London: Article 19, 1995), para. 10, http://www1.umn.edu/humanrts/instree/johannesburg.html#12.

185. The Johannesburg principles are exhaustively detailed but generally they require any restriction on freedom of expression to be narrowly and specifically defined by law. For instance, expressions "intended to incite imminent violence" is one of the few types of speech deemed appropriate for government restriction.[265] That type of speech contrasts sharply with mere criticism or exposure of corruption.

186. The Johannesburg Principles states that restrictions on free expression in the name of national security are only legitimate if:

> its genuine purpose and demonstrable effect is to protect a country's existence or its territorial integrity against the use or threat of force, or its capacity to respond to the use or threat of force, whether from an external source, such as a military threat, or an internal source, such as incitement to violent overthrow of the government.[266]

187. Principle Two goes on to state explicitly what actions should not be used as justification for squelching reporting or other speech. A restriction is not legitimate if its:

> genuine purpose or demonstrable effect is to protect interests unrelated to national security, including, for example, to protect a government from embarrassment or exposure of wrongdoing, or to conceal information about the functioning of its public institutions, or to entrench a particular ideology, or to suppress industrial unrest.[267]

188. While these principles are normative in nature, many governments attempt to abide by them in spirit.[268] Such an approach allows for the freest possible public sphere where ideas can be debated without fear of repercussions.

189. Several areas of UAE law deal with prohibitions of speech and journalistic reporting when dealing with matters of public order and national security. Prohibitions for both public order and national security can be found in the Penal Code, 1980 Press and Publications Act and the 2012 Cybercrime Law. The penalties for these provisions include fines and imprisonment.

190. Article 169 of the Penal Code provides for punishment and fine for providing "news, information, things, correspondence, documents, maps, drawings, pictures, coordinates or any other thing" pertaining to the governmental departments or any other public officials to any foreign state or anyone working in their interests.[269]

191. Article 170 of the Penal Code criminalizes the disclosure of any "military, political and economic" information that must remain secret for "the interest of the state."[270] The article lists various types of documents that must not be divulged and includes specifically information about the armed forces. Part IV of Article 170 also

---

265. *Ibid.*, para. 31.
266. *Ibid.*, para. 26.
267. *Ibid.*, para. 25.
268. Crook, *Comparative Media Law and Ethics.*
269. *United Arab Emirates Penal Code.*
270. *Ibid.*

criminalizes reporting and "news and information" about the arrest of any offenders and information about the trial if the judge makes such a demand.

192. Article 197 of the Penal Code provides for imprisonment and a fine for anyone who uses any type of publicity to publish "any information or news, or to instigate the commission of acts liable to endanger the state security or prejudice the public order."[271]

193. The 1980 Press and Publication Act contains several provisions regarding national security or public order. Article 71 prohibits publication of anything that "causes harm to the interest of the state or the values of society."[272] Article 72 states that "no opinions shall be published if they violate public discipline and order, or involve insult to teenagers, or call for or circulate subversive ideas."[273] The article appears aimed at protecting youth from ideas that incite rebellion. Article 73 states that "any material is absolutely prohibited from being published, if it instigates criminal activity or incites hatred or provokes action of dissension among individuals of society."[274] This article appears aimed at all residents and may also speak to some of the differences between the Sunni and Shiite Muslims as well as the Muslim and Christian faiths.[275]

194. Article 74 of the Press Law bans publication of "confidential official or military communications unless permission is obtained from the proper authority at the ministry,"[276] The article also prohibits the publications of "conventions or treaties the government holds before they are published in the official gazette unless permission is obtained."[277] Article 81 prohibits publication of anything that could "damage to the national economy."[278] Article 98 bans publishing anything that causes harm to the supreme interests of the country, or publishes materials that:

> cause(s) damage to the constitution, particularly to the concept of unity and federation, or threatens public order, or serves foreign interests that contradict national interests, or if the newspaper is discovered to receive any form of assistance from a foreign country, or publishes ideas of a hostile country, or discloses military secrets, or publishes materials that cause confusion among the public.[279]

195. Note that the 1980 Press Law applies to all audio and visual media in the UAE, according to a 2010 clarification from the NMC.[280]

---

271. *Ibid.*
272. *Ibid.*
273. *Ibid.*
274. *Ibid.*
275. The United Arab Emirates is overwhelmingly Sunni Muslim. However, a small population of Shiite Muslims of Persian and Arabic heritage lives in the country because of its historic and current trading ties with Shiite Iran, which sits across the Arabian Gulf.
276. *United Arab Emirates Penal Code.*
277. *Ibid.*
278. *Ibid.*
279. *UAE: 1980 Press and Publications Act.*
280. *Resolution of the Chairman Regarding the Media Content Criterion.*

196. The Cybercrime Law of 2012—which applies to all digital communication—contains several national security and public order provisions. The penalties in the Cybercrime Law tend to be harsher than found in the Penal Code or Media Law. The law often calls for "temporary imprisonment" which is defined in Article 66 of the Penal Code as three to fifteen years in prison.

197. Article 24 prohibits publishing through any electronic means anything that would "promote or praise any programs or ideas which would prompt riot, hatred, racism, sectarianism, or damage the national unity or social peace or prejudice the public order and public morals."[281] The penalty for violation of the provision is temporary imprisonment (three to fifteen years) and a fine of no less than AED 500,000 (USD 135,000) and no more than AED 1 million (USD 270,000).

198. Article 28 provides penalties for spreading through any electronic method any "information, news or cartoon drawings or any other pictures which may endanger the national security and the higher interests of the State or afflicts its public order."[282] The penalty includes temporary imprisonment (three to fifteen years) and a fine of up to AED 1 million (USD 270,000).

199. Article 29 of the cybercrime law criminalizes publishing:

> information, news, statements or rumors on a website or any computer network or information technology means with intent to make sarcasm or damage the reputation, prestige or stature of the State or any of its institutions or its president, vice-president, any of the rulers of the Emirates, their crown princes, or the deputy rulers of the Emirates, the State flag, the national peace, its logo, national anthem or any of its symbols.[283]

200. The penalty for violating any of these prohibitions is temporary imprisonment (three to fifteen years) and a fine of up to AED 1 million (USD 270,000). The article appears grounded as a policy to preserve public order.

201. In a more explicit bid to protect public order and national security, Article 30 makes it illegal to make any calls via electronic means "to overthrow, change the ruling system of the State or seize it or to disrupt the provisions of the constitution or the laws applicable in the country."[284] The article also prohibits opposing "the basic principles which constitutes the foundations of the ruling system of the state."[285] The law also punishes anyone incites or facilitates others to make similar calls. The penalty is "life imprisonment," defined as at least fifteen years in Article 66 of the Penal Code.

202. Article 31 makes it illegal to call via electronic means for others to disobey laws and regulations. The penalty is an unspecified period of imprisonment and/or no less than a fine of AED 200,000 (USD 54,000). Article 32 criminalizes "planning, organizing, promoting or calling for demonstrations or protests or the like without

---

281. *UAE Cybercrime Law of 2012.*
282. *Ibid.*
283. *Ibid.*
284. *Ibid.*
285. *Ibid.*

license from the competent authority."[286] The penalty includes an unspecified length of imprisonment and/or a fine of no more than AED 1 million (USD 270,000).

203. Article 42 allows for deportation of foreigners who are convicted of any of the cybercrime statute's criminal acts. As with other legal punishments in the UAE, the deportation would occur after any prison sentence is served or fine is paid.

204. As demonstrated above, the UAE legal system places many restrictions on journalists and other free expression in the name of public order and national security. The cybercrime law was widely criticized by international organizations although few people in the country spoke out against it. HRW said the cybercrimes law "effectively closes off the country's only remaining forum for free speech. The decree poses a serious threat to the liberty of peaceful activists and ordinary citizens alike."[287]

§4. Blasphemy

205. The Penal Code, Press Law, and Cybercrimes Law contain penalties for blasphemy with the latter two specifically banning content via publication or electronic means. Article 35 of the cybercrime law (similar to the other two) calls for penalties to anyone who commits any of the following crimes:

(1) Insult to any of the Islamic sanctities or rituals.
(2) Insult to any of the sanctities or rituals of other religions where these sanctities and rituals are inviolable pursuant to the provisions of Islamic Sharia.
(3) Insult to any of the recognized celestial religions.
(4) Condoning, provoking or promoting sin.

206. The penalty for violating these provisions is an unspecified prison term and a fine of between 250,000 and AED 1 million (USD 67,500 and USD 270,000). The Cybercrime law carries far higher fines for blasphemy than the other two laws.

207. The imprisonment penalty in the cybercrime law is increased to up to seven years:

> if the crime contains any insult to the Divinity (Allah, God) or to the messengers and prophets or be against the religion of Islam or injures its basis and principles which constitute its foundation, or whoever oppose or injures the well-known teachings and rituals of Islamic religion or prejudices the religion of Islam or preaching another religion or calls for, praises or promotes a doctrine or a notion which involves any of the aforementioned.[288]

208. Blasphemy law violations are not reported in the local press often, but some observers have suggested that they may be abused to settle personal disagreements

286. *Ibid.*
287. "UAE: Cybercrimes Decree Attacks Free Speech," para. 1.
288. *United Arab Emirates Cybercrime Law*, 2012, http://www.scribd.com/doc/120536757/UAE-Cybercrime-Law-of-2012.

rather than protect religions from blasphemy. In 2008, three Filipino workers in Sharjah were accused of blasphemy by one of their co-workers amid a dispute at work. The co-worker was accused of ripping pages from the Koran and writing on them.[289] In another case, an Egyptian man was accused of posting the offensive Mohammad cartoons on his Facebook account. He was also said to have posted pictures of women in bikinis and questions about the Koran. A court psychologist later found him "mentally unstable" which helped ameliorate the punishment.[290]

§5. False News

209. Laws banning the spread of "false news" or other erroneous information sound noble and well-intentioned, however many international courts and legislatures have found such legislation to conflict with free expression and a robust press.[291] The truth can be a contested matter and prohibitions on publishing false news can be abused in an attempt to suppress undesirable allegations, regardless of their truth.[292]

210. Many international courts have recognized the need to protect false news in order to guarantee freely functioning press systems. For instance, the Peruvian Constitutional Tribunal has ruled that the right to freedom of expression encompasses inaccurate statements. The case involved a radio station prosecuted for allegedly disseminating false statements and thereby causing a financial panic. The court refused to intervene saying doing so would breach the station's rights. However, they allowed the plaintiff to seek a correction of the information or pursue the case through the civil courts as a defamation charge.[293]

211. Similarly, the Ugandan Supreme Court struck down a criminal offense of publishing erroneous news. The court noted:

> [T]he right to freedom of expression extends to holding, receiving and imparting all forms of opinions, ideas and information. It is not confined to categories, such as correct opinions, sound ideas or truthful information … [A] person's expression or statement is not precluded from the constitutional protection simply because it is thought by another or others to be false, erroneous, controversial or unpleasant … . Indeed, the protection is most relevant and required where a person's views are opposed or objected to by society or any part thereof, as "false" or "wrong".[294]

289. "Blasphemy: Three Filipinos in Jail in Sharjah, and One Turk Faces Death in Gedda."
290. "Blaspheming Facebooker Is 'Unfit'," *7 Days in Dubai*, accessed June 23, 2012, http://www.7daysindubai.com/Blaspheming-facebooker-unfit/story-15882708-detail/story.html.
291. Buckley et al., *Broadcasting, Voice, and Accountability*.
292. Buckley et al., *Broadcasting, Voice, and Accountability*, 136.
293. Buckley et al., *Broadcasting, Voice, and Accountability*.
294. "Uganda: *Obbo and Another v. Attorney-General* (2004) AHRLR 256 (UgSC 2004)," *Centre for Human Rights: University of Pretoria*, para. 18, accessed December 23, 2012, http://www.chr.up.ac.za/index.php/browse-by-subject/486-uganda-obbo-and-another-v-attorney-general-2004-ahrlr-256-ugsc-2004.html.

212. Most other countries with developed media freedoms similarly do not enforce laws that attempt to penalize journalists for "false news."

213. The UAE government prohibits the publishing or spreading of erroneous news in the Penal Code, Press and Publications Act, and the Cybercrime Law.

214. Article 265 of the Penal Code prohibits publishing information that inaccurately reflects the events in open court. The law criminalizes "any individual who, with his honesty and in bad faith publishes, through any means of publicity, what has taken place during the hearings in open court."[295] The penalty for such a violation is also up to one year of imprisonment and a fine of up to AED 10,000 (USD 2,700). In 2013, the article was used against an activist who was tweeting details of the sedition trial against ninety-four Emiratis.[296] International media outlets had been barred from covering the trial so residents and observers had to rely upon the local press for coverage leading. Some observers, therefore, found Twitter as the only unfiltered source of information.[297] Abdullah Al Haddidi, a son of one of the ninety-four accused of sedition, was sentenced to ten months in jail for violating Article 265.[298]

215. The 1980 Press and Publications Law contains phrases that prohibit the spreading of false news. Article 75, for instance, states that "minutes of meetings, deliberations, or court hearings shall not be published in bad faith, misinterpreted, or distorted."[299] While such a rule seems rooted in upholding good standards of journalism, the question of deciding what report is a "distortion" is essentially a law banning false news. Violators of this prohibition may have their media outlet shut down for up to one year if the cabinet of ministers agrees. They are also subject to up to six months in prison and a fine of up to AED 5,000 (USD 1,350).

216. Article 80 of the Press Law states that it "prohibited to publish in bad faith any false news about someone, or forge or tamper documents to relate them to such individual."[300] This provision appears to provide the same protection that defamation laws (with a specific provision for truth as a defense) would provide. This article also allows for the news outlet to be shuttered for one year as well as a fine of up to AED 5,000 (USD 1,350) and up to six months in prison.

217. Article 82 of the Media Law could also be interpreted to prohibit false news. It states that "publications or advertisements shall not include any phrases, expressions or pictures that are inconsistent with public conduct, or otherwise mislead the public."[301] This law prohibiting publications from misleading the public would require a determination from a government official to decide which information is "true." Part of Article 82 would apply toward commercial advertisements, a regulation widely enforced internationally. (For more on regulation of advertisements, *see* Part

---

295. *UAE Penal Code.*
296. Matt Duffy, "UAE Arrests Activist For 'False News' Tweets," *Al Monitor*, March 27, 2013, http://www.al-monitor.com/pulse/originals/2013/03/twitter-arrest-uae-social-media-law-trial.html.
297. *Ibid.*
298. "UAE Activist Jailed for Court Tweet," *BBC*, April 8, 2013, http://www.bbc.co.uk/news/world-middle-east-22071517.
299. *UAE: 1980 Press and Publications Act.*
300. *Ibid.*
301. *Ibid.*

II, Chapter 4). Violators of Article 82 face up to six months in prison and a fine of AED 5,000 (USD 1,350.)

218. And the updated Cybercrime Law of 2012 also prohibits false news. Article 29 states that publication of "rumors" on a website or through any electronic means is prohibited. The determination of what constitutes a "rumor" could be highly subjective and essentially represents a ban on false news. Penalties for violating this article are temporary imprisonment (three to fifteen years) and a fine of up to AED 1 million (USD 270,000).

219. Article 38 of the cybercrime law of 2012 criminalizes the spreading through electronic means "any incorrect, inaccurate or misleading information which may damage the interests of the State or injures its reputation, prestige or stature."[302] Such an edict therefore bans the dissemination of false news, despite the dangers that such a law poses to freedom of expression. The penalty for violation is temporary imprisonment, defined in the Penal Code as three to fifteen years.

§6. Prohibition of Insults

220. The prohibition of insults is increasingly seen as incompatible with free and open communication. Many observers see insult legislation and prosecution as incompatible with a free and well-functioning press because of the nebulous nature of the charge and the ease with which it may be abused to stifle legitimate criticism.[303]

221. Many countries have decriminalized these offenses or simply choose to avoid prosecutions even through insult laws are still on the books.[304] In the U.K. efforts are underway to repeal the insult law of 1986 even though it's only been enforced a handful of times.[305] In the meantime, the police recently clarified that no one in the country will be arrested for "insulting" comments on Twitter except when some type of violence is suggested.[306]

222. Insults are prohibited in several different laws of the UAE. The issue of defamation (damaging someone's reputation through spoken or written words) is often linked with insults, a more nebulous legal concept. In no part of the laws analyzed here is a specific definition of "insult" offered.

223. Bans against insults in the UAE are often coupled with defamation charges. Article 20 of the Cybercrime Law of 2012 makes it a crime for "whoever insults or accuses another person of a matter of which he shall be subject to punishment or being held in contempt by others" while using digital communications.[307] Slander or an insult committed toward a public official is considered an aggravating factor. The punishment is an undefined prison term and a fine of between AED 250,000 (USD 67,500) and

302. *United Arab Emirates Cybercrime Law.*
303. Buckley et al., *Broadcasting, Voice, and Accountability.*
304. McCracken, *Insult Laws: Insulting to Press Freedom.*
305. "Why Insults Are a Political Issue," *The Guardian*, May 16, 2012, http://www.guardian.co.uk/law/2012/may/16/why-insults-are-political-issue.
306. Dominic Casciani, "*Prosecutors Clarify Offensive Online Posts Law*," *BBC*, December 19, 2012, sec. UK, http://www.bbc.co.uk/news/uk-20777002.
307. *UAE Cybercrime Law of 2012.*

AED 500,000 (USD 135,000). Making an insult to a public figure an aggravating factor creates a situation in which public figures are protected from insulting speech more than private figures. Such an approach differs from many countries in which public figures receive fewer protections against libel than private counterparts. This approach allows for the widest possible discourse on matters involving the public interest (for more, *see* Defamation and Libel above.)

The Penal Code does not contain the word "insult," however the local press has referred to insult charges. Police are apparently using the defamation provisions, such as, Article 372, which prohibits "through any means of publicity charges another person with an incident susceptible of making him subject to punishment or exposing him to public hatred or contempt."[308] In 2007, a court fined a business manager AED 5,000 (USD 1,350) for insulting a colleague by cursing at him.[309] And in 2013, a woman received a fine of AED 1,000 (USD 270) for insulting her friend's former husband by calling him 'stupid' in front of a police officer.[310]

§7. Lese-Majeste Laws (Insulting the Ruler)

224. Several countries still hold onto *lese-majeste* laws (French for 'injured king') that date back to Roman times and essentially prohibit any speech that may offend the king or ruler of a country. Critics note that these laws' broad definition can be used to suppress critical speech against the government.[311] Many nations—particularly those that have evolved into constitutional monarchies—have eliminated their *lese-majeste* laws or simply no longer enforce them.[312]

225. The UAE, like most of the Gulf monarchies, feature legislation that criminalizes criticism aimed at the country's rulers.

226. Article 70 of the 1980 Press and Publications Act enforces a *lese-majeste* law: "No criticism shall be made against the Head of State or Rulers of the Emirates."[313] Violators face a fine of up to AED 20,000 (USD 5,400) and a prison sentence of between six months and two years. Such a broad restriction against criticism of the leader of the country can have far-reaching effects on reporting.

227. Article 29 of the Cybercrime Law updated in 2012 also contains broad prohibitions on communication that could insult the rulers of the Emirates. The article criminalizes the publication of:

308. *UAE Penal Code.*

309. Bassem Za'za', "Court Gives Manager Dh5,000 Fine for Insulting Man," *Gulf News*, June 30, 2007, http://gulfnews.com/news/gulf/uae/crime/court-gives-manager-dh5-000-fine-for-insulting-man-1.186230.

310. Salam Al Amir, "Woman Fined Dh1,000 by Dubai Court for Calling Man Stupid," *The National*, May 12, 2013, http://www.thenational.ae/news/uae-news/courts/woman-fined-dh1-000-by-dubai-court-for-calling-man-stupid.

311. McCracken, *Insult Laws: Insulting to Press Freedom*; Ruth Walden, *Insult Laws: An Insult to Press Freedom* (Reston, Va.: World Press Freedom Committee, 2000), http://www.wpfc.org/site/docs/pdf/Insult%20Laws-Text.PDF.

312. Streckfuss Davi, *Truth on Trial in Thailand: Defamation, Treason, and Lèse-majesté* (Taylor & Francis, 2011).

313. *UAE: 1980 Press and Publications Act.*

information, news, statements or rumors on a website or any computer network or information technology means with intent to make sarcasm or damage the reputation, prestige or stature of the State or any of its institutions or its president, vice-president, any of the rulers of the Emirates, their crown princes, or the deputy rulers of the Emirates, the State flag, the national peace, its logo, national anthem or any of its symbols.[314]

228. Violators may be imprisoned for an unspecified length of time and fined up to AED 1 million (USD 270,000.) These broad restrictions on speech that may "damage the reputation" or "prestige" of a ruler could lead to self-censorship on the part of journalists.

229. Articles 176 and 8 of the UAE Penal Code make it a crime to publicly insult the UAE's rulers.[315] Article 176 states that "any person who insults by any means of publicity the President of the State, its flag or its national emblem shall be punishable by confinement for a period not exceeding five years."[316] Article 8 makes any reference in the Penal Code to the president apply equally to the vice-president, the rulers of the seven emirates and their crown princes and their deputies. This portion of the law and several others were used to prosecute several online activists during a period of upheaval across the region in 2011.[317] The activists were also charged with endangering national security and inciting protests.[318] (*See* Part I, section 6 for more on this case.)

§8. Corrections and Right of Reply

230. The concept to a "right of reply" refers to the reservation of space in a news outlet for an aggrieved party to respond to a piece of journalism they feel was inaccurate or misleading. When news outlets make mistakes, corrections are published or broadcast to admit the error and correct the record.

231. Internationally, countries have differed over whether to make "right of reply" compulsory with media outlets. In the United States, for instance, the U.S. Supreme Court has ruled that such a demand is an undue burden on the freedom of the press.[319] Similarly, Canada and the U.K. do not compel the media to offer corrections or right of reply, relying instead upon the news media to develop their own self-regulation to enforce high standards of conduct regarding instances of inaccurate or misleading reports. However, many countries in Europe, South America, and elsewhere

314. *UAE Cybercrime Law of 2012.*
315. *UAE: End "travesty of Justice" for Five Convicted over President Insults | Amnesty International.*
316. *UAE Penal Code.*
317. Barbara Surk, "5 UAE Convicted Reform Activists Freed from Jail," *Boston.com*, November 28, 2011, http://www.boston.com/news/world/middleeast/articles/2011/11/28/uae_president_pardons_5_convicted_activists/.
318. "Five Emiratis Arrested for Threatening UAE Security," *The National*, April 26, 2011, http://www.thenational.ae/news/uae-news/five-emiratis-arrested-for-threatening-uae-security.
319. "Miami Herald Publishing Co. V. Tornillo," *Casebriefs*, 1974, http://www.casebriefs.com/blog/law/constitutional-law/constitutional-law-keyed-to-cohen/freedom-of-the-press/miami-herald-publishing-co-v-tornillo/.

do use limited legislation to compel responsive and responsible news media. According to one international Media Law text, best practices for "right of reply" statutes include the following:

(1) A reply should be required only in response to statements that are false or misleading and that breach an important interest of the claimant. Replies are not permitted for opinions that are disliked.
(2) A reply should receive similar placement and length as the original article or broadcast.
(3) A reply should only address incorrect or misleading facts in the original text.
(4) Media should not be required to carry abusive or illegal reply.[320]

232. Articles 40 through 43 of the Press and Publications Act of 1980 involve the publishing of corrections and their judicial review. The law states that a "proper authority" may demand corrections for previous reports that are published.[321] The term "proper authority" is never defined, but the law makes it appear that anyone may bring such a complaint, so the authors probably intended public officials to make use of these provisions. The law mandates that these corrections must be published in the next issue following the demand and be printed in the same place and font size as the original report. These corrections must be published free of charge if space is not more than double the original article. If the correction exceeds this length then the proper authority will pay for the excess space. If the editor of a newspaper refuses to publish the correction, an unspecified judge can examine the issue. If the judge rules against the editor, he or she may be sent to jail for six months and fined up to AED 10,000 (USD 2,700). If the court acquits the editor, he may insist the newspaper publish a different wording of a correction. If the editor is sentenced, he may still abstain from printing the correction. However, the "plaintiff" in the case may publish the correction in three other newspapers and bill the editor who was found guilty. If the editor wins the case, he can publish his victory "at the expense of the client." Given that the aggrieved party can apparently write the "correction," these articles allow for "right of reply," although this term is not used specifically.

§9. Avoiding Names in Press Coverage

233. Press outlets in the UAE generally do not put the name of accused criminals in their reports. Instead, crime stories will often feature just the initials of the accused and usually their nationality. Even after criminals have been convicted of a crime, UAE news outlets generally avoid identifying criminals.

234. The practice appears to be linked to the country's strict defamation laws and Article 263 of the Penal Code. The Penal Code article prohibits publishing any information which may sway a judge or notably to affect "the public opinion in favor of or against any of the parties in a case or investigation." Article 264 of the Penal Code contains a long list of prohibitions regarding publishing information related to

320. Buckley et al., *Broadcasting, Voice, and Accountability*, 152.
321. *UAE: 1980 Press and Publications Act.*

court cases, but not naming suspects in a crime is not mentioned. (*See* Part I, section 4 for more on the Penal Code restrictions.)

235. Defamation laws also play a role in the withholding of names in crime stories. The online website Emirates 24/7 (owned by a Dubai government holding company) explains on the "editorial policy" section of its website:

> When we only print the initials of individuals involved in court cases it is because they are part of an ongoing case. Consequently, under UAE law, it is considered to be prejudicial to name them and the newspaper can be sued. The individuals can only be named in full once the court has given its verdict and the timeframe allowed for an appeal has expired.[322]

236. It is unclear if the website is referring to "prejudicial" in terms of the Penal Code or defamation laws. Waiting until a criminal had exhausted all remedies at exoneration would clear either legal requirement. In practice, UAE press outlets rarely go back and identify anyone convicted of a crime even after the appeals process is exhausted. This deference may be due to the clear lack of truth as a defense for libel as well as to the cultural norms surrounding the importance of reputation in the Arab world. A blow to one person's reputation reflects on the entire family and, in some cases, the family's tribe.

237. In many countries (such as the United States or the United Kingdom), defamation laws do not protect residents who have been accused of a crime because the charges are public record and truth can be used as a defense for defamation, even if the publicity surrounding an arrest damages their reputations. In other countries (such as Norway and Sweden), names are withheld as a journalistic tradition but not due to a lack of legal protection.[323]

238. An interview with a long-time journalist in the UAE helped shed light on this situation. The journalist, who wished to remain anonymous because of the sensitivity of the subject matter, said that fear of defamation laws generally prompted the withholding of names. However, the journalist pointed out that in practice some criminal suspects are identified. The journalist pointed to a case in which a newspaper ran the photo and name of a criminal after the police sent the information to the press. Other cases have also seen the press publish names after the government press agency released them. The case of the "UAE5," for instance, saw newspapers publish the names of all five defendants accused of insulting the president and other crimes after the Emirates News Agency released the information.[324] The names were published months before court proceedings against the five ended in their conviction and presidential pardon.

239. Press outlets have also identified the names of some suspects in high-profile cases involving foreign defendants. For instance, one newspaper identified the American

322. "Editorial Policy," *Emirates 24/7*, para. 8, accessed January 7, 2013, http://www.emirates247.com/editorial-policy-1.153.
323. Maggie Jones Patterson & Romayne Smith Fullerton, "*Naming Names: Crime Coverage Rituals in North America, Sweden, and the Netherlands*," in *Association for Education in Journalism and Mass Communication* (St. Louis, MO, 2011), http://citation.allacademic.com/meta/p_mla_apa_research_citation/5/2/0/1/6/p520168_index.html.
324. "Five Emiratis Arrested for Threatening UAE Security."

businessman who has been jailed in Dubai since 2007 over business debts.[325] The case has received widespread coverage in the regional business press.

§10. Case Studies

240. The following section details several incidents and court cases involving media coverage in the UAE. These examples should help provide a foundation for further understanding the media regulations in the country.

I. Shaikh Issa bin Zayed al Nahyan Case

241. The media coverage of a 2009 case in which a member of the ruling family was accused of torture provides a foil for observing the media landscape of the UAE. Sheikh Issa bin Zayed al Nahyan, the President's brother and one of nineteen sons of the founder of the country, was caught on videotape torturing an Afghani merchant whom he believed had cheated him in a business deal. The tape was smuggled out of the country and aired by ABC News in the United States.[326] Coverage of the video made international news and led to a debate in the U.S. Congress about the country's relationship with the UAE, particularly because of a nuclear energy knowledge-sharing agreement. The local media effectively ignored the videotape and international outcry despite the intense foreign media coverage.[327] Sheikh Issa was eventually exonerated of criminal charges in a courtroom in Al Ain, the ruling family's ancestral hometown, in a ruling widely criticized by international observers.[328]

242. A report on National Public Radio offered insight into the local media system, noting that even The National newspaper, with its stable of Western journalists, avoided reporting in any detail on the case.[329] Even after the state news agency, WAM, issued a statement saying that the government would investigate the charges, The National and other local media still ignored the report. Usually, the local media will report on "sensitive" stories after the state news agency issues a statement. So, the avoidance of the story even after the WAM publication led to speculation that the statement was prepared for foreign journalists only and the NMC had instructed the

325. Salam Al Amir, "Former Deyaar Chief Zack Shahin Back in UAE Custody," September 2, 2012, http://www.thenational.ae/news/uae-news/former-deyaar-chief-zack-shahin-back-in-uae-custody.
326. Vic Walter et al., "Torture Tape Implicates UAE Royal Sheikh," *ABC News*, April 22, 2009, http://abcnews.go.com/Blotter/story?id=7402099.
327. Kelly McEvers, "Outrage Over Torture Video Goes Unheard In UAE: NPR," *NPR.org*, May 23, 2009, http://www.npr.org/templates/story/story.php?storyId=104498602.
328. "Issa Bin Zayed Al Nahyan, Abu Dhabi Royal, Acquitted In Torture Trial (VIDEO)," *Huffington Post*, January 11, 2010, http://www.huffingtonpost.com/2010/01/11/sheik-issa-bin-zayed-al-n_n_418978.html.
329. McEvers, "Outrage Over Torture Video Goes Unheard In UAE."

local press to ignore it.[330] No one from the The National would comment publicly about the decision.[331]

243. The NMC's Director-General, Ibrahim al Abed, said that the avoidance of coverage had more to do with culture than media laws. "(Critics) don't understand the culture," he told a foreign journalist. "If you are part of the culture, you feel this is nothing. It's something taken for granted. Nobody will ridicule the president or … the ruling family".[332] Of course, the laws do provide penalties for insulting or defaming members of the ruling family. Therefore, the avoidance could have more to do with the legal and regulatory environment than simply the prevailing culture.

II. Defamation Case of Hetta Online Magazine

244. In 2010, the Abu Dhabi Court of Cassation exercised its right according to the 1980 Press and Publication Act to close a website after a defamation ruling. The case stemmed from an article in the privately owned online magazine, Hetta.com, about Abu Dhabi TV, the government-owned news and entertainment channel. The case revolved around an article by Enas Borini under the headline "Abu Dhabi TV: Emirate TV only in name" which criticized the way the station's channels were being administered. The chairperson of Abu Dhabi Media Company, the government-owned parent company of the television station, filed defamation charges against the magazine. The article alleged the company featured "administrative corruption" and "embezzlement" and criticized the Abu Dhabi television station's programming. The defamation charges officially stemmed not from the article but from comments posted online by members of the audience. A lower court and the appeals court ruled against the online news outlet and its editor, Ahmad Mohammed bin Gharib.[333]

245. Some observers noted that the criminal defamation charges were filed rather than making a simple request to the owners of the website to remove the offending comments.[334] They also noted that the article generated many comments, a sign that the subject matter was deemed interesting to the public. The Arabic Network for Human Rights Information (ANHRI) had pleaded with the appeals court to overturn the conviction on the grounds that the UAE had made recent progress in protecting freedom of expression with Sheikh Maktoum bin Rashid's decree ending the jailing of journalists. ANHRI also lamented the effect of the ruling would have on the freedom of expression from commenters (who would likely face far more stringent filtering) and on future online magazine articles.[335]

330. *Ibid.*
331. El-Baltaji, "Arab Media & Society."
332. McEvers, "Outrage Over Torture Video Goes Unheard In UAE," para. 16.
333. *In Support of Freedom of Expression ANHRI Calls the UAE Judiciary to a Different Legal Approach to Handle the Case of Chief Editor of "Hetta" E-magazine* (The Arabic Network for Human Rights Information, October 10, 2009), http://www.anhri.net/en/reports/2009/pr1010.shtml.
334. *Ibid.*
335. *Ibid.*

246. In early 2010, the Appeals Court upheld the conviction and closed the website for one month. The court also fined the editor AED 20,000 (USD 5,400) plus AED 10,000 (USD 2,700) in damages paid to Abu Dhabi Media Company. Prosecutors brought the charges by citing defamation provisions in three different laws: Article 372 of the Penal Code, Articles 79 and 86 of the 1980 Press and Publications Act, and Article 16 of the Cybercrime Act of 2006.[336]

247. Observers noted that government-owned telecom companies blocked access to the website before the legal procedures were completed.[337] The case appeared to "have been orchestrated with the aim of intimidating and silence silencing independent journalists."[338]

248. The case offers a notable example in which powerful figures (the director of a television station and chairperson of a government-owned media corporation) used defamation laws to effectively discourage independent reporting and public discussion.

III. Defamation Case of Emarat Al Youm

249. A 2006 article in the Arabic-language daily newspaper Emarat Al Youm ("Emirates Today") resulted in a fine and suspension of the newspaper for twenty days.[339] The case stemmed from an article that accused Warsan Stables of giving steroids to horses during a race in Abu Dhabi. Members of Abu Dhabi's royal family own the Warsan Stables while the Dubai government's media holding company, Dubai Media, owns Emarat al Youm.[340] Despite its government ownership, the newspaper is known for its critical journalism and often independent perspective.

250. The incident was referred to as a defamation case but reports never indicated exactly which laws were violated. The Penal Code, 1980 Press and Publications Act and 2006 Cybercrime Law all contain defamation provisions. The prosecuting attorney in the case, Ammar al Khaja, said the newspaper was given a year to "prove the story was true."[341] The issue of truth as a defense for libel is murky in the UAE. Some provisions of defamation law appear to allow for such a defense (Article 372 of the Penal Code) while other defamation provisions (Article 20 of the cybercrime law of 2012 and Article 70 of the Press and Publications Act of 1980) do not specify whether

---

336. "Authorities Bend Rules to Block Access to Online Magazine," *Reporters Without Borders*, July 2, 2010, http://en.rsf.org/united-arab-emirates-court-closes-independent-website-14-01-2010,36104.html.
337. *Ibid.*
338. RWB, *Authorities Bend Rules to Block Access to Online Magazine - Reporters Without Borders*, para. 1.
339. Abdullah Rasheed, "Emarat Al Youm Suspended as of Today," *Gulf News*, July 5, 2009, http://gulfnews.com/news/gulf/uae/media/emarat-al-youm-suspended-as-of-today-1.500173.
340. "UAE Suspends Newspaper over 'Horse Doping' Claims," accessed December 31, 2012, http://www.arabianbusiness.com/uae-suspends-newspaper-over-horse-doping-claims-16392.html.
341. Loveday Morris, "Arabic Daily Suspended over Horse-doping Libel," *The National*, July 3, 2009, para. 2, http://www.thenational.ae/news/uae-news/arabic-daily-suspended-over-horse-doping-libel.

truth absolves the defendant in a libel case. (For more discussion on this issue, *see* section 1 above on defamation and libel.)

251. The case ended in 2009 when the Abu Dhabi Federal Court of Appeals upheld a Supreme Federal Court ruling against the newspaper. The court issued a fine of AED 20,000 (USD 5,400) against Emarat al Youm's editor Sami Al Riyami, and its publisher, Abdul Latif Al Sayegh, the chairman of the Arab Media Group (which owned the newspaper before Dubai Media.) The court also ordered the suspension of the newspaper for twenty days, a penalty allowed under Article 88 of the 1980 Press and Publications Act of 1980.[342]

252. The order to suspend came from the country's media regulation agency, the NMC. The Attorney-General's Office sent the suspension order to the NMC after the court's ruling.[343]

253. The Chairman of the UAE Journalists' Association, Mohammad Yousuf, said they were disappointed with the suspension of the newspaper, particularly because of an apparent move toward more press freedoms in the country. A decree in 2007 had effectively ended the practice of jailing journalists for offenses.

254. Yousuf said suspension of a newspaper should not be one of the penalties meted against press outlets. He suggested that only four liabilities should be held in cases of opinion expression and publishing: correction, apology, fine, and compensation. Those four remedies can be found in the 1980 Press Law in addition to jail and suspension.

255. Reporters Without Borders and the International Federation of Journalists both criticized the closure of the newspaper.[344]

IV. Coverage of the Sedition Trial in 2013

256. In 2013, security forces in the country detained scores of Emiratis over the summer without explanation. After several months of detention without charges, federal prosecutors charged ninety-four suspects with the crime of sedition, attempting to overthrow the government. Many of the suspects were accused of speaking out on social media to call for democratic reform in the United Arab Emirates. They were accused of being aligned with the "Al Ishah" movement, a branch of the Muslim Brotherhood, a group officially banned in the UAE.

257. The government banned the foreign press from the trial, a move that limited the reports of the court proceedings. Accounts of the trial were only disseminated to through the self-censoring local press. During the trial, police arrested at least three Emiratis in attendance who had tweeted trial proceedings. The Emiratis reported on defense criticisms about the general lack of due process and complaints that prosecutors were not providing their evidence. The arrested Emiratis were accused of spreading "false news" about the trial and were charged with violations of the penal code and

342. Rasheed, 'Emarat Al Youm Suspended as of Today.'

343. *Ibid.*

344. 'Newspaper Suspended for 20 Days over Story Race Horse,' *Reporters Without Borders*, July 7, 2009, http://en.rsf.org/united-arab-emirates-newspaper-suspended-for-20-days-07-07-2009,33730.html; Rasheed, 'Emarat Al Youm Suspended as of Today.'

cybercrime law.[345] At the trial's conclusion, a total of sixty-nine of the ninety-four suspects were convicted of sedition. (All those released were women.) Those found guilty received sentences of up to fifteen years in prison.[346] Human rights groups said the trial was unfair and lacked due process.[347]

V. The Obaid Al Zaabi CNN interview

258. In 2013, an Emirati gave an interview to the global news network CNN in which he criticized the lack of free speech in the UAE. In an example of extra-legal actions taken by the enigmatic security forces, he disappeared immediately following the appearance on television. After seven months in detention with no charges, prosecutors brought formal charges of "offending the Supreme Court," "offending the state security apparatus" and "instigating people against the rulers and the security of the state."[348] Al Zaabi's court trial ended in a not guilty verdict, observers said, because of his poor health.[349] However, after the verdict, he was not released from detention. According to one Emirati, the security services are keeping him in a hospital ward because they are "worried if they release him he will go active on the online media again."[350] The ignored verdict shows that the security forces act outside the legal system to exercise censorship and intimidation.

VI. Other Defamation Cases

259. Criminal defamation laws were also used against British journalist accused of posting defamatory information against his former employer, the Khaleej Times, a newspaper in Sharjah. According to a report from the Media Legal Defense Initiative, the case went on for twenty-two months despite scant evidence linking him to the defamatory post on an Internet forum. The journalist was eventually exonerated in 2011, but he was forced to surrender his passport and remain in the UAE for nearly two years without work until the case finally ended.[351]

260. The defamation laws have also effectively hamper reporting on issues surrounding unethical business practices in the UAE. Buyers unhappy with their property developers' lack of progress reported being worried of criminal defamation

345. http://www.al-monitor.com/pulse/originals/2014/03/twitter-cybercrime-uae-activists-prison-law.html.
346. http://www.thenational.ae/uae/courts/uae-sedition-trial-69-guilty-25-cleared-as-all-accused-women-walk-free-from-court.
347. https://www.hrw.org/news/2013/04/03/uae-unfair-mass-trial-94-dissidents; https://www.amnesty.org/en/press-releases/2014/01/uae-end-downward-cycle-unfair-political-trials/.
348. https://www.amnestyusa.org/sites/default/files/f2u34113.pdf.
349. http://www.al-monitor.com/pulse/originals/2014/07/uae-twitter-imprisoned-not-guilty-activist-cyber-crime.html.
350. *Ibid*, para. 11.
351. MLDI, *British Journalist Wins Two Year Criminal Libel Ordeal in Dubai* (London: Media Legal Defence Initiative, June 22, 2011), http://www.mediadefence.org/news-story/british-journalist-wins-two-year-criminal-libel-ordeal-dubai.

charges if they voiced their concerns publicly or to the press. In one case, a lawyer faced criminal charges for making a statement about a developer at a public forum. The case ended in acquittal but the lawyer had to surrender his passport and wait a year for adjudication. Observers point to the absence of truth as a defense to criminal defamation charges as having a sizable impact on both free expression and press freedom.[352]

261. In 2007, a court in the northern emirate of Ra's al-Khaimah sentenced the owner of a website, majan.net, to a year in prison and a fine for the defamation of a local official. The court also ordered the site to be closed, apparently through the provision for such a move in the 1980 Press and Publications Act. A writer for the website was also charged with defaming and insulting a physician who worked for the health ministry. The news and forum website had outlined charges of corruption and mismanagement in the health ministry. Both sentences were eventually overturned on appeal after the public official who brought the charges dropped the charges. Both the owner of the website and the writer spent several months in jail while awaiting adjudication.[353]

262. In 2011, a Dubai criminal court fined an Emirati radio and television broadcaster AED 10,000 (USD 2,700) for defaming and insulting a preacher during his live show on the radio. The radio broadcaster had accused the claimant of being fired from his job on his own local show because he discussed sexual education in Islam. The judge also allowed a civil claim for AED 21,000 (USD 5,670) in damages to proceed. Local press reports did not indicate whether the truth of the defamatory statement was used as a defense.[354]

263. In 2013, an American was arrested after he and several others (including two Emiratis) created and posted a satirical video on YouTube. Shezanne Cassim and the others were sentenced for one year in prison for allegedly "threatening UAE security and endangering public order" with the video that mocked affluent youth in Dubai who enjoy pampered lifestyles while mimicking gang behavior. He and the other defendants were released after nine months.[355] The police apparently charged the men with Article 29 of the expanded 2012 cybercrime law that prohibits "sarcasm or damage (to) the reputation, prestige or stature of the State."[356]

264. In 2013, a video recorded in Dubai that showed an Emirati beating an Indian expatriate shed light on the UAE's defamation provisions. The video showed the aftermath of a wreck in which an Emirati driver berated and whipped a man who was involved. The video lasted for several minutes until another person intervened. After being uploaded to YouTube and seen by several hundred thousand viewers, police arrested the Emirati man for the assault. A few days later, the Emirati's family

352. Brass, "Defamation Laws Keep the Aggrieved Quiet."
353. *Court Closes Libel Case Against Website Reporter* (Paris, France: Reporters Without Borders, December 3, 2007), http://en.rsf.org/united-arab-emirates-court-closes-libel-case-against-03-12-2007,24444.html.
354. Bassam Za'Za, "Broadcaster Fined Dh10,000 for Defaming Preacher," *Gulf News*, May 25, 2011, http://gulfnews.com/news/gulf/uae/crime/broadcaster-fined-dh10-000-for-defaming-preacher-1.812541.
355. http://www.theguardian.com/world/2013/dec/23/american-one-year-sentence-uae-satirical-video.
356. http://www.wipo.int/wipolex/en/text.jsp?file_id=316909.

had the person who uploaded the video arrested on criminal defamation charges. After a few days, charges against both the Emirati and the Indian expat were dropped after the agreement of both parties. The incident shows that even the truth of videotaped incident did not provide a defense against a defamation charge.[357]

357. http://www.al-monitor.com/pulse/originals/2013/07/emirati-assault-video-defamation.html.

Chapter 4. Advertising Regulations

265. Regulations of advertisements in the UAE come mainly from the 1980 Press and Publications Act (and its enforcer, the NMC) as well as consumer protection regulations. Many countries approach media regulation in the same manner although some nations, such as the U.K., also employ a self-regulating advertising standards body.

266. The enforcement of the regulations vary depending on media and locality. In practice, some advertisers seek approval for their ads ahead of time from various authorities. For example, the NMC could prohibit "inappropriate" television advertising or Dubai Municipality may object to an outdoor advertisement that violates regulations.[358]

§1. Press and Publication Act Regulations

267. The 1980 Press and Publications Act—which applies to all media in the UAE—contains two provisions specifically aimed at the regulation of advertising.

268. Article 82 prohibits advertisements containing any phrases, expressions or pictures that are "inconsistent with public conduct."[359] Such a prohibition allows for ads to be deemed inappropriate for public consumption (e.g., featuring models dressed too immodestly for the conservative country.) The NMC provides input on these decisions through its "media monitoring service" that provides "permissions for the circulation and production" of advertisements.[360]

269. Article 82 also prohibits ads that mislead the public. The section reads: "Publications or advertisements shall not include any phrases, expressions or pictures that are inconsistent with public conduct, or otherwise mislead public."[361]

270. Most countries enforce laws that prohibit false advertising. The general approach toward such regulation is from a perspective of fraud. In essence, governments protect consumers from making purchases based on false facts. In these cases, the seller has created a breach of contract by not delivering a good or service as promised.

271. Article 83 states that "no advertisements shall be made on medicines, or pharmaceutical preparations unless by permission from the proper authority at the Ministry of Health." The Ministry of Health has also been given oversight of tobacco advertising and other substances deemed a public health concern.[362]

272. Parts of the Media Law would also apply to advertising, particularly sections on respecting the local culture by publishing or broadcasting offensive material. For instance, Article 71 prohibits any material that may cause "harm to the interest of the state or the values of society."[363] Article 72 could also limit some types of advertising:

358. Michael Lunjevich, "Comparative Advertising in the UAE," August 4, 2009, http://www.hadefpartners.com/News/pageid/120-137/default.aspx?mediaid=78.
359. *UAE: 1980 Press and Publications Act.*
360. "Our Services."
361. *UAE: 1980 Press and Publications Act.*
362. Hamid, "National Media Council Tells Advertisers to Keep Their Lingo Local - The National."
363. *UAE: 1980 Press and Publications Act.*

"No opinions shall be published if they violate public discipline and order, or involve insult to teenagers, or call for or circulate subversive ideas."[364]

§2. Consumer Protection Laws

273. Restrictions on false advertising can also be found in the UAE's business regulations. The Consumer Protection Law, Federal Law No.(24) of 2006, created many aspects of protection for consumers in the UAE including to prohibit false advertising and provide a remedy for such cases.[365]

274. The Executive Regulation of the Consumer Protection Law (1993) specifically provides: "No person shall be permitted to advertise in any medium any goods or service in such manner leading to deceiving or confusing consumers."[366] Another regulation, the Suppression of Fraud Executive Regulation, also addresses indirect or direct commercial speech. It holds that all advertisements "must be accurate in all respects whether placed on products, shops, inside shops or on packaging, invoices, correspondence, advertising material or other things used to offer good to the public."[367] Violators of these provisions face both fines and imprisonment.

§3. National Media Council Regulations

275. In 2013, the NMC issued a statement regarding advertising content regulations that stressed the "fundamental ethics" for advertisers in the UAE. The NMC instructed advertisers to respect the "religion, cultural and social values and norms in society."[368] It pointed to regulations and laws that already addressed advertising as well as the code of ethics from the Emirates Journalists Association, which also addresses respecting cultural norms.

276. The NMC also instructed advertisers to use a specific form of Arabic in their communication—either standard Arabic or the local Emirati dialect. One industry observer called the move to ban the other dialects (such as Egyptian or Lebanese) "unusual."[369] The NMC clarified this point by noting that the regulation only applies to television advertisements being made in the UAE for transmission in the country. The regulation would not apply to an advertisement made in Beirut in a Lebanese accent and transmitted in the UAE.[370]

364. *Ibid.*
365. Waldo Steyn, *Advertising Regulations in the UAE* (Al Tamimi & Company, September 12, 2012), http://www.tamimi.com/en/publication/publications/section-3/september/advertising-regulations-in-the-uae.html.
366. *Ibid.*, para. 7.
367. *Ibid.*, para. 10.
368. WAM, "National Media Council Issues Advertising Content Regulation," *Breitbart.com*, January 16, 2013, para. 1, http://www.breitbart.com/system/wire/upi20130116-123010-2998.
369. Triska Hamid, "National Media Council Tells Advertisers to Keep Their Lingo Local," *The National*, January 17, 2013, para. 3, http://www.thenational.ae/thenationalconversation/industry-insights/media/national-media-council-tells-advertisers-to-keep-their-lingo-local.
370. Hellyer, Personal Communication.

277. The statement from the NMC also reminded advertisers about other advertising prohibitions such as:

- Tobacco and related products.
- Alcoholic beverages.
- Mind-altering substances.
- Witchcraft or occult.

278. The statement also stressed that advertisers should respond to complaints or criticisms in a prompt fashion.[371]

371. Hamid, "National Media Council Tells Advertisers to Keep Their Lingo Local."

Part III. Supervision: Media Regulator

§1. National Media Council Oversees All Media

279. In many countries, regulatory duties are split up between print and broadcast journalism. In the U.S., for instance, the Federal Communications Commission (FCC) regulates the broadcast airwaves and plays a limited role in regulating cable and internet distribution. However, the FCC does not regulate print newspapers or online news media at all—nor does any other federal body. Most European countries, South Korea, Japan, and other developed nations also avoid having a centralized regulator for print and online media.[372] In many countries some type of independent, self-regulating "press council" will hear complaints about the print media and take actions that can include fines.[373]

280. The reason for the demarcation between print and broadcast regulation lies in the pervasive nature of the broadcast medium as well as the scarcity of airwaves. Governments have generally chosen to regulate broadcasts because of worry over inappropriate content that could potentially harm society—particularly children—as well as the need to allocate frequencies to specific broadcasters so that signals would not overlap. Broadcast television regulations are generally set up to be "content neutral," so that journalistic independence is not violated.

281. The NMC—a federal government agency—regulates all print, radio, television, and digital content in the UAE.[374] A resolution passed in 2010 said the Press and Publications Act of 1980 applied to all "visible, audible and legible" media.[375] According to the NMC's website, the agency was established by Federal Law (1) for 2006 following amendments to Federal Law (91) for 1972 regarding ministries' and ministers' mandates and specializations. The agency's mandates include supervising the media as determined by the myriad of regulations described in the 1980 Press Law or implementing any instructions from the federal cabinet (the heads of the federal ministries) or other regulations or laws. The NMC states that its vision is "to reach international standards in media regulation to achieve sustainable development in the

372. Glasser, *International Libel and Privacy Handbook*.

373. Bill Ristow, *Sword and Shield: Self-Regulation and International Media* (Washington, D.C.: Center for International Media Assistance), accessed January 24, 2013, http://cima.ned.org/publications/research-reports/sword-and-shield-self-regulation-and-international-media.

374. The Telecommunications Regulation Authority overseas the regulation of the Internet as well. However, the 2010 resolution from the National Media Council chairman specifically notes that the 1980 Press and Publications Act apply to.

375. *Resolution of the Chairman Regarding the Media Content Criterion.*

UAE."[376] The agency's stated goals are to create a "regulatory environment conducive to the development of the media sector" and to highlight "UAE accomplishments at national and international levels."[377]

282. Using the word "council" in the agency's title lends itself to comparisons with the press councils found in Europe and other countries with free media environments. These press councils are independent, self-regulating institutions set up to raise ethical standards and offer a centralized organ for complaints about the media. The NMC is a government agency that officially enforces the laws of the 1980 Press and Publications Act and effectively acts as a censor on the nation's media.

§2. Not Completely Transparent

283. The website for the NMC notes that the agency "promotes attitudes and conducts based on transparency and honesty." Unfortunately, the NMC itself lacks in transparency, helping to add a nebulous nature to the regulation environment. Its website includes a section called "Media Laws and Regulations," but only two English-language documents appear on it: The 1980 Press Law and the 2002 Copyright Law. The following documents (discovered during research for this book) are not available in English on the website:

(1) Resolution of the Chairman Regarding the Media Content Criterion of 2010 regarding the primacy of the 1980 Press Law and its application to all media.
(2) Cabinet Resolution No.14 of 1999 regarding the fees for media licenses of commercial nature.
(3) Cabinet Resolution No.14 of 2006 and its amendments regarding the NMC regulation.
(4) Cabinet Resolution No.70/13 of 2007 regarding the practice of some free zone areas to media licenses.
(5) Cabinet Resolution No.38 of 2008 regarding the organization chart of the NMC.[378]
(6) Details released in 2013 regarding the regulation of advertising.[379]

284. After inquiries were made about these documents, the NMC uploaded some of them to the English portion of the website, despite the fact that they are written in Arabic.[380]

285. The exact nature of the NMC's oversight is ambiguous. In a 2011 interview in Dubai's Gulf News, the NMC Director-General Ibrahim Al Abed said:

---

376. "About Us," *National Media Council*, 2012, para. 5, http://nmc.gov.ae/en/Pages/AboutUs.aspx.
377. *Ibid.*, para. 9.
378. The preceding four documents are cited in the 2010 resolution from the National Media Council chairman.
379. Triska Hamid, "National Media Council Tells Advertisers to Keep Their Lingo Local - The National," *The National*, January 17, 2013, http://www.thenational.ae/thenationalconversation/industry-insights/media/national-media-council-tells-advertisers-to-keep-their-lingo-local.
380. "Media Laws And Regulation," *National Media Council*, accessed May 12, 2013, http://nmc.gov.ae/en/pages/MediaLawsAndRegulation.aspx.

> Since its establishment in 2006, the NMC has been keen on building up solid relations with the local press through meetings to discuss mutual concerns and problems. So, far this working relationship has proven to be most effective in facilitating local media contribution to national development.[381]

286. Al Abed's description refers to meetings with editors of the local for discussions but not the delivery of any specific instructions. In fact, he later says clearly that the NMC never issues specific directives: "As always, the way in which the media exercise the freedom that they have is largely up to them—the NMC cannot demand that they do so."[382] Personal discussions with the news media professionals suggest that such direct orders are a rarity, although some pointed to the local coverage a 2009 incident involving a member of the ruling family as an example in which such direct instructions were issued.[383] With that incident (described in detail in Part II, section 10), the official news agency released a statement that was picked up by the foreign press but notably ignored by the local press. Some observers speculate that the NMC had directly ordered the local press not to publish the statement that was intended to merely appease foreign critics.[384]

287. Usually the NMC's regulation is subtler. The agency also operates the Emirates News Agency (known by its Arabic initials WAM). The news agency allows the NMC to effectively provide guidance for "sensitive" stories. Oftentimes, news outlets will not run controversial reports—such as arrests of residents over security concerns—until WAM has issued its own. One journalist decried the current system of ambiguous regulation, arguing it would be better if:

> there were someone in the room from the government saying, 'You can say this and not that.' At least then everyone would know where they stood. But the truth is that government intervention is applied retrospectively. It means you don't know exactly where you stand so you must err on the side of caution.[385]

288. The suggestion shows that the NMC and other factors leads to an atmosphere of ambiguity that prevents journalists from operating with more independence.

289. In 2013, The Nation magazine detailed a rare instance of communication between the NMC and one of the local press outlets.[386] The magazine detailed that the NMC director-general wrote a letter to the newspaper's editor Hassan Fattah complaining about two features in the newspaper's weekend section.[387] One was a travel piece on

---

381. Rasheed, "Freedom and Responsibility Go Together to Secure State's Interest," para. 3.
382. Abdulla Rasheed, "Freedom and Responsibility Go Together to Secure State's Interest," *Gulf News* (Dubai, February 22, 2011), para. 3, http://gulfnews.com/news/gulf/uae/media/freedom-and-responsibility-go-together-to-secure-state-s-interest-1.765596.
383. McEvers, "Outrage Over Torture Video Goes Unheard In UAE."
384. El-Baltaji, "Arab Media & Society."
385. Sam Potter, "Financial Crisis in the UAE - A Paralysis of Analysis," *Arab Media & Society*, Spring 2010, 2, http://www.arabmediasociety.com/topics/index.php?t_article=286.
386. "Ukraine: TV Channel Finds Itself Under Hostile Fire In Fight For Country's Presidency," News, *RadioFreeEurope*, October 22, 2004, http://www.rferl.org/featuresarticle/2004/10/790dcfb1-4279-4c90-9145-357970930849.html.
387. The author has also obtained a copy of the NMC letter.

visiting Nazareth, Israel, and the other was a profile piece on Israel's Intelligence Chief. The UAE, along with the Gulf states and several other Arab countries, does not recognize the state of Israel. "Both pieces reflect, in my view, the fact that many of your editors still completely fail to understand in real terms where they are living," wrote Ibrahim Al Abed, the director-general of the NMC. "It is time that they came to recognize that what might be acceptable in newspapers elsewhere is not necessarily suitable for a UAE audience—or for a newspaper owned by the Government of Abu Dhabi."[388] The article noted the editor of that section was released from his job after the articles were published.[389]

290. The NMC lists several services on its website including issuing licenses for media outlets, the accreditation of journalists operating in the UAE, and providing news feeds from the Emirates News Agency.

291. The agency also offers "monitoring media content" that includes "permissions for the circulation and production of wide-ranging media contents in the print and audio-visual forms."[390] This appears to refer to pre-approval of material that a publisher or broadcaster may find questionable.

292. In 2013, the chairman of the NMC issued a resolution forming a consultative council for the agency. The council is made up of officials from media institutions and academics and tasked with discussing, following up and coordinating on joint initiatives with media outlets. The group also reviews topics and makes recommendations to the chairman.[391]

388. Joe Pompeo, "'We Are Not Here to Fight for Press Freedom'," *The New Republic*, February 28, 2013, http://www.newrepublic.com/article/112542/national-abu-dhabis-brief-experiment-press-freedom#.

389. *Ibid.*

390. "Our Services," *National Media Council*, accessed January 25, 2013, http://nmc.gov.ae/en/Pages/OurServices.aspx.

391. WAM, "National Media Council Gets Consultative Panel," *Gulf News*, March 21, 2013, http://m.gulfnews.com/news/uae/national-media-council-gets-consultative-panel-1.1161288.

Appendices

Appendix 1: UAE Constitution, Articles on Freedom of Expression

Article 30

Freedom of opinion and expressing it verbally, in writing or by other means of expression shall be guaranteed within the limits of law.

Article 31

Freedom of communication by post, telegraph or other means of communication and the secrecy thereof shall be guaranteed in accordance with law.

Appendix 2: UAE Penal Code: Sections on Defamation, Privacy

Article 8

All the provisions contained herein regarding the crimes committed against the President of the State shall also be applicable to the crimes committed against the State Vice President, the members of the Federal Supreme Council, their crown princes and deputies.

Article 176

Any person who insults by any means of publicity the President of the State, its flag or its national emblem shall be punishable by confinement for a period not exceeding five years.

Article 263:

Shall be punishable by confinement or by fine any individual who publishes, through any means of publicity, any matters with the intention of causing influence on the Judges—to whom the power of decision is granted concerning a case lodged with them—or on the members of Public Prosecution, any other persons who are charged with the investigation or expertise, or an any witness who may be called upon to testify in any case or investigation. Shall also be liable to the same penalty, he who publishes, through any means of publicity, any matters with the intention of hindering a person from declaring any information to the competent authorities, or of influencing the public opinion in favour of or against any of the parties in a case or investigation.

In the event where the published matters are false, the offender shall be punishable by confinement and by fine.

Article 264:

Shall be punishable by confinement for a period not exceeding one year or by a fine not exceeding ten thousand Dirhams any individual who, through any means of publicity, publishes:

1. Information concerning a current investigation of a Case or any of such investigations documents, if the investigation authority has interdicted the publication of any part thereof.
2. Information concerning the investigations or procedures in Cases of kinship, marriage, guardianship, divorce, alimony, separation, adultery, slander or divulgence of secrets.
3. Names or pictures of accused juvenile delinquents.
4. Names or pictures of victims in crimes committed against honour.
5. Names or pictures of convicts with stay of execution of the punishment.
6. Deliberations of Courts and Tribunals.

7. Information concerning the cases which the Courts have decided to try in secret session or have interdicted their publication.

Article 265:

Shall also be liable to the same hereinabove specified punishment any individual who, with his honesty and in bad faith publishes, through any means of publicity, what has taken place during the hearings in open court.

Article 312:

Shall be punishable by confinement and by fine or by one of these two penalties any individual who commits any of the following offences:

1. Offence against any of the Islamic sacred things or rites.
2. To insult and revile any of the recognized divine religions.
3. To portray disobedience in a positive light, to incite thereto, to promote it or to procure any mean susceptible of tempting people to disobey.
4. To knowingly eat porkmeat while being a Muslim.

Article 372

Shall be punishable by confinement for a period not exceeding two years or by a fine not exceeding twenty thousand Dirhams any individual who, through any means of publicity charges another person with an incident susceptible of making him subject to punishment or exposing him to public hatred or contempt. The punishment shall be confinement and a fine or one of these two penalties if the act of libel is committed against a public officer or any person to whom a public service is assigned, during the performance of his function or public service, due to or on the occasion of such performance; or if the act of libel violates the honour or takes from the reputation of families, or if it is noticeable that the act is intended for the attainment of an unlawful objective.

In the event where the act of libel is expressed by publication in newspaper or printed matters, this shall be considered a circumstance of aggravation.

Article 373:

Shall be punishable by confinement for a period not exceeding one year or by a fine not exceeding ten thousand dirhams any individual who makes, through any means of publicity, a false accusation which dishonors or discredits a man in estimate of public, without imputing any specific incident to him.

The penalty shall be confinement for a period not exceeding two years and a fine not exceeding twenty thousand Dirhams in the two cases, or one of these two penalties if the act of slander is committed against a public officer or a person to whom a public service is assigned, during the performance of his function or public service, due to or on the occasion of such performance, or if the act of slander violates the honor or takes from the reputation of families, or if it is noticeable that the act is intended for the attainment of unlawful objectives. In the event where the act of slander is expressed by publication in newspaper or printed matters, this shall be considered a circumstance of aggravation.

Article 374:

A punishment of confinement for a period not exceeding six months or a fine not exceeding five thousand dirhams shall be inflicted if libel or slander occurs over the telephone, or in the presence of the victim and of a third party.

The punishment shall be a fine not exceeding five thousand Dirhams if libel or slander is committed against the victim in nobody's presence or by a letter sent to the victim or by any means whatsoever. The circumstance shall be considered aggravating if the libel or slander in the cases given in the two preceding paragraphs is committed against a public officer or a person entrusted with a public service, during the performance of his function or public service, due to or on the occasion of such performance, or if the offense violates the honor or offends the reputation of families, or if it is noticeable that the act is intended for the attainment of unlawful objectives.

Article 375:

There is no crime if the offender proves the reality of the incident which he imputed to the victim, whenever such incrimination is performed against a public officer or a person to whom a public service is assigned and whenever the said incident is connected with the function or service.

In such a case, slander may also be proved if it were committed by the offender personally and were connected with the incident of libel.

However, evidence may not be brought if more than five years have already elapsed since the happening of the incident, if the crime was extinguished for any cause of extinguishment or if the judgment pronounced, deciding the criminal case, has abated.

Article 376:

In respect of oral or written statements made by a party in his defence (whether before the Courts or any investigating bodies), no crime shall be imputed for the maker of the statement (whether by defamation or slander) within the limits of a party's right of defence.

Article 377:

There is no crime if an individual informs in good faith the judicial or administrative authorities of an act for which its author is answerable.

Appendices, Appendix 2: UAE Penal Code: Sections on

Article 378

Where any of the above offences is committed in public, the punishment shall be either confinement for a minimum period of one year or a fine.

A punishment of confinement and fine shall be inflicted on any person who attacks the sanctity of individuals' private or family life by committing any of the following acts in other than the legally permitted cases or without the victim's consent:

A. Eavesdropping or recording or transmitting by any system of whatever kind any conversation held at a particular place or via the phone or any other set.

B. Picking up or transmitting by any system of whatever kind a person's picture at a particular place.

If the acts referred to in the above two cases during a meeting within the hearing or sight of the person attending, their consent shall be required. The same punishment shall be inflicted on any person who publishes through any means of publicity news, pictures or comments pertaining to the secrets of people's private or familial lives even if the same is true.

A punishment of confinement for a period not exceeding seven years and a fine shall be inflicted on any public officer who commits any of the acts described in this article depending on his functionary authority.

In all cases, systems and other tools used in the crime shall be confiscated and the recordings found shall be obliterated or destroyed.

Article 379:

Any individual who, by reason of his profession, craft, circumstance or art is entrusted with a secret and who discloses it in cases other than those permitted by the law, or who uses it for his own advantage or another person's advantage, shall be punishable by imprisonment for a minimum period of one year and by a fine of at least twenty thousand dirhams (or by one of these two penalties) unless the individual to whom the secret pertains has consented that it be disclosed or used.

The punishment shall be imprisonment for a period not exceeding 5 years if the perpetrator is a public servant or an officer entrusted with a public service to whom the secret has been confided during, because or by reason of performing his duties or services.

Article 380:

Shall be punishable by a fine of at least three thousand Dirhams any individual who opens a letter or telegram, without the consent of the addressee, or he who eavesdrops a telephone conversation. Said offender shall be punished with confinement for a minimum period of three months or with a fine of at least five thousand Dirhams if he discloses the letter, telegram or telephone conversation to any person other than the addressee without his consent, whenever such disclosure is susceptible of causing prejudice to third parties.

Appendix 3: Print and Publications Law, Complete

Chapter 1—Definitions

Words and expressions used in this document are defined as under unless stated otherwise

Article 1

State: The United Arab Emirates
Ministry: The Ministry of Information and Culture
Minister: Minister of Information and Culture
Publications: All written material, drawings, musical compositions, or any other form of expression that can be heard or viewed. Circulation: Selling, distributing publications or displaying them for the purpose of sale or advertisement, or any other action that makes publications within the reach of a number of people.
Newspaper: Any newspaper, a magazine, or a publication, issued regularly or intermittently under one name.
Printing press: Equipment or system for printing or recording words, drawings or pictures for the purpose publication and circulation. The phrase does not apply to cameras, normal typing machines or photocopiers.
Owner of the printing press: Applies to anyone leasing the printing press.
Publisher: Anyone who publishes printed material.
Bookshop: Any establishment that trades in all types of publications.
Works: Literary, artistic and scientific works in whatever form.
Cinema: Any work that features visual means of expression.
News Agency: Any press establishment that disseminates pictures or words through tickers, telegraphic machines or any other means.

Chapter 2
Printing Presses and Publications

Article 2

Owner or the manager of a printing press shall fulfil the following requirements:

1. He shall be a UAE national
2. He shall be fully qualified.
3. He shall be of good conduct and must not have been convicted for an offence involving moral turpitude, or he has been acquitted or his moral standing has been restored by the proper authority.

Article 3

No one is allowed to operate a printing press unless he obtains a licence as per provisions of this law.

Application for a licence shall be submitted to the Department of Information and Publications at the ministry, and shall include the following details:

1. Name of the printing press owner.
2. Name of the manager who runs the printing press, his surname, nationality and place of residence.
3. Name of the printing house, its location and type of tools used and their number.

Article 4

The proper authority at the ministry shall approve or not approve the application within thirty (30) days of the date the application is submitted.

Any delay beyond this date shall be considered acceptance of the application.

Article 5

In case the application is rejected, a complaint against the decision can be submitted to the minister within fifteen (15) days of the date the application was rejected.

The minister shall take a decision on the complaint within fifteen (15) days and his decision shall be considered final.

Article 6

The owner of the printing press or the official responsible shall notify inwriting the proper authority at the ministry of any change to the details of the application for licensing. The matter shall be brought to the attention of the authority within fifteen (15) days of the date the change is made.

Article 7

The owner of the printing press shall waive ownership of his printing press only to a UAE national, who fulfils requirements mentioned in Article 2 of this law and after prior approval in writing from the proper authority at the ministry. The assigner shall submit to the proper authority an application including all details and documents confirming conditions mentioned in Article 2 of this law, and these are required from the assignee.

Article 8

If the owner of the printing press dies, his heirs shall notify the ministry in writing of his death within two months (2) of the death. The printing press licence shall go to the heirs, unless they express their desire to discontinue the printing press activity. This is made without prejudice to provisions of Article 2 of this law.

Article 9

The owner of the printing press or its manager shall keep a record stamped by the ministry, to record titles of material pending publishing, names of the material originators and number of copies printed from that material.

The owner or the manager shall submit the record to the proper authority at the ministry.

Article 10

The name of the printing house and its address shall be recorded clearly in one of the pages of the printed material and also the name of the publisher and his address.

Article 11

Ten copies of the published material shall be submitted by the printing house to the censorship department at the ministry.

Article 12

An approval from the proper authority at the ministry shall be obtained by the printing house before any journal is published. The authority shall take a decision on the application submitted within fourteen (14) days of the date the application is submitted.

Article 13

Provisions of Articles 10, 11, and 12 of this law shall not apply to publications of a private or commercial nature.

Article 14

The printing house, before printing any material ordered by any party which does not hold UAE nationality, shall obtain permission from the proper authority at the ministry to print that material. The authority shall issue a decision on the application for permission within fourteen (14) days of the date the application is submitted.

Article 15

The printing house shall neither reproduce any material for circulation in the country, which is prohibited by the proper authority, and nor shall it print any material that contradict Articles 12 and 14 of this law.

Article 16

The printing house shall obtain permission from the proper authority at the ministry if a customer orders material to be printed for the purpose of distribution in another country. Application for permission shall include the material ordered to be printed, the name of the customer, his nationality and his place of residence.

Chapter 3
Circulation of Publications

Article 17

No one is allowed to sell, or distribute publications on the main road or in any public place, even temporarily, unless he obtains permission from the proper authority at the ministry.

Article 18

Anyone who wishes to sell or distribute publications shall register his name with the proper authority at the ministry. The minister shall issue a decision explaining the rules of registration.

Article 19

Publishers and suppliers of publications shall submit to the proper authority at the ministry five (5) copies of each publication they publish or supply before they circulate such publications. One copy of each publication is required if only a few copies of such publications are imported. Copies submitted shall be returned after procedures are completed. The minister shall issue a decision specifying such publications.

In all cases, a receipt shall be issued for copies submitted.

The authority mentioned in the first paragraph shall, without delay, issue a decision with respect to circulation of the publications. The authority may delete from the publication any paragraph including material whose circulation is prohibited by the provision of this law. Deletion may be made by cutting out the subject material by scissors, or covering details by a special ink or any other tools deemed effective. In case the deletion is impossible, the minister may prohibit circulation of the publication in the country.

Article 20

The minister may ban any periodical or any publication from entering the country if that publication includes material prohibited to be circulated by the provisions of this law or any other law.

Decisions issued by the minister shall be published in the official gazette and as per provisions of the previous paragraph.

Article 21

Parties are prohibited to circulate any imported publication unless they obtain permission from censorship department at the ministry.

Article 22

No diplomatic missions in the UAE is allowed to issue any publication for the purpose of circulation unless they obtain permission from the proper authority at the ministry. Application for permission shall be submitted through official channels and must include a draft of the publication stamped by the head of the diplomatic mission. In case the circulation of the publication is approved five (5) copies of the publication shall be submitted to the proper authority at the ministry before it is circulated.

Article 23

Clubs, societies or foreign centres are not allowed to issue or circulate any publication unless permission is obtained from the proper authority at the ministry. Application for permission shall include a draft of the publication stamped by the head of the club, society or centre. If permission is issued, five (5) copies shall be submitted to the proper authority at the ministry before the publication is circulated.

Provisions of the previous paragraph apply to publications of private or commercial nature.

Chapter 4
Newspapers, Periodicals, and News Agencies

Article 24

No newspaper shall be published unless permission from provisions of this law is obtained.

Article 25

The owner of the newspaper shall meet the following requirements:

1. He shall be a UAE national. This requirement shall not apply to periodicals issued by diplomatic missions and foreign news agencies licensed to operate in the UAE.
2. He shall not be less than 25 years of age.
3. Shall be fully competent.
4. He shall be of good conduct and behaviour.
5. He shall not have been previously convicted for an offence involving moral turpitude, or unless he has been acquitted or his moral standing has been restored by the proper authority.
6. He shall not occupy a public service post in the country.
7. He shall not be employed by a foreign agency in the country.

Article 26

Any newspaper shall have an editor-in-chief to supervise its entire content, or it shall have a number of editors, each of whom supervises a particular section. Owner of a newspaper may be the editor-in-chief of his newspaper or a responsible editor if he meets requirements provided in this law.

Article 27

The editor-in-chief or the editor shall meet the following requirements:

1. Shall hold a higher degree from a recognised college, institute or university.
2. He shall have scientific experience not less than one year, with full experience to perform his job.

Article 28

Any editor or writer wishing to work in a newspaper shall meet the following requirements:

1. He shall have a higher scientific degree from a recognized college, institute, or university, or otherwise, he shall have practised journalism regularly for not less than three years.
2. He shall have been registered with the authorities organising the journalistic profession in his country.
3. He shall be fully qualified.
4. He shall not have been previously convicted of an offence involving moral turpitude, unless he is acquitted or his moral standing has been restored by the proper authority.
5. He shall not have been previously ordered to leave the country for an offence related to publishing.
6. He shall not hold a job with a foreign country or agency.
7. He shall not be a public servant.

The two requirements included in clauses 1 and 2 shall not apply to UAE nationals.

Article 29

Newspaper owners and chairmen of boards of journalistic establishments and news agencies shall not appoint editors or writers on a permanent or temporary basis, unless they are registered with the information department in the ministry.

Provisions included in the previous paragraph shall not apply to foreign correspondents appointed by their agencies abroad. Individuals and agencies mentioned in paragraph 1 shall notify the proper authority at the ministry of the names of foreign correspondents, their nationalities and place of residence.

Article 30

Foreign correspondents are prohibited to practise their job in the country before they are licensed by the proper authority in the ministry. Licensing shall be for one year, which can then be renewed.

The ministry shall sponsor foreign correspondents.

Article 31

Anyone wishing to issue a newspaper shall submit an application to the proper authority in the ministry including the following details:

1. Name, surname, nationality and place of residence of the applicant.
2. Name of the editor-in-chief or editors and publishers, if any, and their surnames, their age, nationality, place of residence and qualifications.
3. The name of the newspaper, its language, the date of issuance and its address.
4. The name of the printing press in which the newspaper is published if it does not have its own printing press.

The application shall be signed by the newspaper owner, or editor in-chief or by editors or the publisher, if any.

Article 32

The minister shall submit the newspaper's licensing application to the Cabinet to take a decision on it. The application shall be supported by the ministry's own opinion on the subject.

Article 33

The owner of the newspaper or the editor-in-chief shall notify the proper authority at the ministry of any change that occurs to details of the application. The notification shall be made within eight (8) days at the maximum of the date the change is made.

Article 34

The undersigned of the application provided in Article 31, shall deposit along with the application, a guarantee of Dh 50,000 for each daily newspaper, and Dh 25,000 for the other cases. This shall be made to ensure settlement of fines imposed by the provisions of this law or any other law against the editor-in-chief, editors, or the owners of the newspaper, the publishers or the printing press.

The guarantee may be made by a bank guarantee issued by one of the banks operating in the UAE and is payable to the ministry. The guarantee shall be irrevocable and unconditional.

Article 35

The guarantee shall be replenished the fifteen (15) days following a warning served in this respect, if the guarantee provided in the previous article dwindles after fines have been deducted from it.

Article 36

Any printing house is prohibited to print a newspaper, whose license expires, or the proper authority suspends its activity, or it is prohibited from being circulated in the country.

Article 37

No newspaper shall be circulated, unless it includes the name of the owner, editor-in-chief, or the editor, the name of the printing press, its date of issuance, place of issuance, price of an issue, value of subscription. All these details shall be printed clearly either on the front or the last page. If the newspaper has no editor-in-chief, but a number of editors each of whom is responsible for a particular section, their names must be printed in the same way mentioned above.

Article 38

As soon as an issue of a newspaper or its supplement is circulated, five copies shall be submitted to the proper authority at the ministry. Receipts of the copies shall be issued to the newspaper.

If the newspaper issues a number of different copies of the same issue, a copy of each different issue shall be submitted to the ministry.

Article 39

The editor-in-chief or the editor shall publish free of charge any public notices sent by the ministries. Notices shall be published in places where important news is published.

Article 40

The editor-in-chief or the editor shall publish upon the request of the proper authority any correction for news previously published. Correction shall be published in the first issue published following the request and in the same place and with the same font size. These corrections shall be published free of charge if the space it takes is not twice the size of the original article. Fees shall be paid for the excess space.

Article 41

No newspaper shall abstain form publishing any correction, unless in the following cases:

a. If the correction is received two months after the date of publication of the article.
b. If the newspaper has previously published the corrections.
c. If the correction is written in a language other than the language in which the original article is published.
d. If the publishing of the correction entails an offence punishable by the law.

Article 42

If the editor-in-chief or the editor abstain from publishing the correction, he shall be imprisoned for a term not less than six (6) months, and/or pay a fine not less Dh 1000 and not more than Dh 10,000.

Article 43

The court, when it acquits the editor-in-chief or the editor from the charges provided in the previous article may obligate them to publish the correction in any wording it sees suitable.

If the editor-in-chief or the editor is sentenced, the correction shall be published in the first or the second issues following the issuance of the sentence. If the defendant abstains from publishing the correction, the plaintiff may publish the correction in three newspapers of his choice and at the expenses of the defendant.

The editor-in-chief or the editor if he is cleared of the charges leveled against him, may publish that at the expenses of the plaintiff.

Article 44

The owner of the newspaper shall waive ownership of his newspaper only to a UAE national, who meets requirements mentioned in Article 25 of this law and after approval from the proper authority at the ministry. The assigner shall submit to the proper authority an application including all details and documents confirming conditions mentioned in Article 20 of this law and are required from the assignee.

Article 45

The licence of a newspaper is cancelled by a decision by the minister and upon request from its owner. The minister may cancel the licence in the following cases:

1. If the newspaper does not appear within six (6) months of the date the licence is issued.
2. If the newspaper does not appear regularly within six (6) months of the date the licence is issued.
3. If the owner of the newspaper dies and his heirs are not able to issue the newspaper regularly within one (1) year of the date of the owner's death.

Article 46

Newspapers or periodicals shall not copy articles, novels, stories or any other literary work unless there is consent of the author. Quotation, or brief notes may by copied without the consent of the author.

Newspapers may publish articles that discuss political, economic, scientific, or literary issues, or other issues of public interest unless publications of such issues are prohibited.

The author of the article and the source shall be mentioned clearly.

Article 47

Newspapers and periodicals may quote arguments and pleadings that take place in the courts and within the limit set by the law, unless the court decides that the proceedings take place in a closed hearing.

Article 48

Articles 17, 18, and 20 of this law apply to circulation, or selling of newspapers or banning them from entering the country.

Provisions included in Articles 19 and 21 of this law apply to import and circulation of foreign newspapers.

Chapter 5
Import and Export of Publications and Newspapers

Article 49

Non-UAE nationals registered in the record are prohibited to import or export publications and newspapers.

Article 50

No one shall be registered in the records mentioned in the previous article unless he belongs to one of the following categories:

a. Press establishments and firms dealing in publishing.
b. Parties that import or export publications and newspapers.

Article 51

Anyone wishing to be registered in the records mentioned in Article 49 of this law shall submit an application to the proper authority at the ministry accompanied by the following documents:

a. A Declaration of two copies that include the applicant's name, his surname, nationality, place of residence and the name of his press establishment, its location, names of the partners or directors authorised to sign for the firm.
b. Details of offices, where import and export processes take place and the name and surname of owner of each office, his nationality and his place of residence.

Article 52

Anyone registered in the records mentioned in Article 49 of this law shall notify the proper authority of any change made to the details mentioned in the previous article. Notification shall be made within fourteen (14) days of the date of the change.

Article 53

No Holy Quran books, or part thereof, or religious books published in the form of publications or audio material, shall be imported without permission from the proper authority in the ministry and without the prior consent of Ministry of Justice, Islamic Affairs and Awqaf.

In all cases, imported copies shall have been approved by the responsible religious bodies in Arab or Islamic countries.

Chapter 6
Cinema Films and Other Artistic Shows

Article 54

No party shall be allowed to import or export films unless he is a UAE national registered in the records kept by the ministry.

Article 55

Anyone wishing to be registered in the record mentioned in the previous article shall submit an application to the proper authority at the ministry accompanied by the following documents:

c. A Declaration of two copies that include the applicant's name, his surname, nationality, place of residence and the name of his press establishment, its location, names of the partners or directors authorised to sign for the firm.

d. Details of offices, where import and export processes take place and the name and surname of owner of each office, his nationality and his place of residence.

Article 56

Anyone registered in the records mentioned in Article 54 of this law shall notify the proper authority of any change made to the details mentioned in the previous article. Notification shall be made within fourteen (14) days of the date of the change.

Article 57 No film or a commercial advertisement shall be allowed to be shown in a cinema hall unless permission is obtained from the film censorship committee. Documents required to be submitted along with the application shall be determined by a decision by the minister.

Article 58

No diplomatic mission shall be allowed to show a film to individuals other than its employees and in a venue other than its official location unless permission is obtained from the film censorship committee.

Clubs, societies or centres are not allowed to show even to its members and in its official location unless they obtain permission from the committee mentioned in the previous paragraph. Documents required to be submitted along with the application for permission shall be determined by a decision from the minister.

Article 59

A committee referred to as the "Film Censorship Committee" shall be set up and chaired by the ministry's assistant undersecretary for press censorship affairs. Members of the committee shall be representatives of ministries of education; interior, social affairs, justice and Islamic affairs, state security and Israel boycott office. A decision by the minister shall be issued to set up the committee. Ministries' representatives are nominated by their ministries.

The committee shall be assigned to examine films to be shown in cinema halls. The committee is also assigned to examine films that are shown to individuals other than officials of diplomatic missions and in places other than official locations of such missions. The committee examines political, social, moral and religious content of films shown by clubs, societies and centres.

The minister may appoint in the committee anyone with competence and experience.

Article 60

The committee mentioned in the previous article may remove from the film any scene that it sees involving moral turpitude, or violating religious morals or values on which state and society are based.

The committee may permit the film to be shown after the scenes are removed.

The ministry may issue instructions to cinema halls or officials managing such halls to maintain a good standard of films.

Article 61

The Film Censorship Committee shall not license any foreign film to be shown unless there is an Arabic subtitle.

The application for permission shall include a summary of the film, its actors and the name of the producer.

In all cases the Arabic subtitle must conform to the film's dialogue.

Article 62

A committee shall be set up in the ministry and referred to as the "Higher Committee of Grievance". The committee, the members of which will be people from the field of art and law, shall be assigned to look into grievances raised by owners of cinema halls against decisions taken by the Film Censorship Committee and in accordance with provisions of Articles 57, 58, and 61 of this law.

The committee shall be set up by a decision by the minister.

In all cases, the decision of the committee shall be based on logical reasons.

Grievances against the committee's decisions may be submitted to the minister within fifteen (15) days of the date the decision of the committee is issued, and the decision of the minister shall be final.

Article 63

No one, whose age is less than sixteen (16) years shall be allowed to watch a film shown in cinema halls, or any other place specified by a decision by the Minister of Labour and Social Affairs.

Article 64

Managers of cinema halls and other similar places mentioned in the previous article shall issue a notice in a clear place prohibiting children under sixteen years of age from watching the film and as per the decision issued in this respect by the Film Censorship Committee.

Article 65

The minister shall issue a decision naming the ministry's officials authorized to enter cinema halls and other places mentioned in Article 63 and printing presses and places where publications are sold and distributed. The officials will enforce the law and are empowered to confiscate any material or prove any action contradicting requirements of this law. They are empowered to confiscate materials and tools used in committing offences provided in this law.

Article 66

In places other than cinema halls, no artistic work shall be shown to the public without prior permission from the information department of the ministry. Applications for permission shall include details and documents.

Such details and documents are specified by a decision issued by the minister.

Provisions of the previous paragraph apply to circulation or publication of any artistic work, whether such work is audio or visual.

Article 67

No one shall be allowed to perform theatre or screen cinemas, or the like, unless he is licensed by the proper authority at the ministry. Licensing shall be for one year, which can then be renewed. A decision by the minister shall specify requirements of the licence, its renewal and documents required to be submitted along with the application.

Article 68

Provisions of the previous article apply to individuals facilitating employment of cinema and theatre actors, or other artistes.

Article 69

Provisions of Articles 66, 67, and 68 of this law shall not apply to shows sponsored by ministries, government departments and public institutions and which are shown for the purpose of supporting their activities.

Chapter 7
Materials Prohibited to Be Published

Article 70

No criticism shall be made against the Head of State or Rulers of the Emirates

Appendices, Appendix 3: Print and Publications Law,

Article 71

Any work is absolutely prohibited from being published if it involves instigation against Islam or the system of ruling, or if it causes harm to the interest of the state or the values of society.

Article 72

No opinions shall be published if they violate public discipline and order, or involve insult to teenagers, or call for or circulate subversive ideas.

Article 73

Any material is absolutely prohibited from being published, if it instigates criminal activity or incites hatred or provokes action of dissension among individuals of society.

Article 74

It is absolutely prohibited to publish confidential official or military communications unless permission is obtained from the proper authority at the ministry. It is also prohibited to publish conventions or treaties the government holds before they are published in the official gazette unless permission is obtained.

Article 75

Minutes of meetings, deliberations, or court hearings shall not be published in bad faith, misinterpreted or distorted.

Article 76

No article blemishing the president of an Arab, Islamic or any other friendly state will be published. It is also prohibited to publish any material that causes agitation to relations between the UAE and other Arab, Islamic and friendly countries.

Article 77

No article defaming Arabs and their civilisation and heritage shall be published.

Article 78

No news on an ongoing criminal investigation shall be published if the judge orders investigations to be kept confidential, or the public prosecution restricts publication.

Article 79

No news, pictures, comments about an individuals' private life shall be published if their publication is meant to disgrace such individuals. It is also prohibited to disclose any secret that may cause harm to the reputation of someone, or his property, his commercial name, or if the publication is meant to coerce somebody into paying some money or render a benefit to someone else, or the like.

Article 80

It is prohibited to publish in bad faith any false news about someone, or forge or tamper documents to relate them to such individual.

Article 81

It is prohibited to publish news that cause harm to the national currency, or causes damage to the national economy.

Article 82

Publications or advertisements shall not include any phrases, expressions or pictures that are inconsistent with public conduct, or otherwise mislead public.

Article 83

No advertisements shall be made on medicines, or pharmaceutical preparations unless by permission from the proper authority at the Ministry of Health.

Article 84

It is prohibited to malign a public official, or anybody occupying a post in the public prosecution, or assigned to perform a public job. The writer shall not be held responsible if he proves he did so in good faith.

Article 85

No reportage involving more than one person shall be published unless it covers points of views of all parties involved in that reportage.

Chapter 8
Penalties

Article 86

Anyone violating any provision of Articles 24, 26, 27, 29, 33, 57, and 58, or articles from 71 to 85, shall be imprisoned for a term not less than one (1) month and not more than six (6) months and/or fined not less than Dh 1000 and not more than Dh 5000.

The court may, apart from the punishment prescribed by the previous paragraph, suspend the activity of the newspaper, or close down the cinema hall for a period not more than one (1) month.

Article 87

Violators of provisions of Articles 19, 20, 21 of this law are subject to punishment provided in paragraph (1) of the previous article.

Article 88

The owner of the newspaper, editor-in-chief, editors and publishers, if any, shall be imprisoned for a term not less than six (6) months, and/or fined not more than Dh 10,000, if they issue the newspaper after it closed down, even if it was issued under another name.

The court may, apart from the punishment included in the previous paragraph, suspend the activity of the newspaper for a period of not more than two (2) months.

Article 89

Any violator of provisions of Article 70 of this law shall be imprisoned for a term not less than six (6) months and not more than two years and/or fined not less than Dh 5000 and not more than Dh 20,000. The editor-in-chief shall be punishable by punishment provided in the previous paragraph.

The court may, apart from the punishment included in the two previous paragraphs, suspend activity of the newspaper for a period of not more than six (6) months.

Article 90

Published material or the newspaper may be administratively impounded if publication, issuance and circulation are made in violation of provisions of Articles 12, 14, 15, 16, 20, 21, 22, 23, 24, 36, 37 and 44 of this law. The matter shall be brought to the court to decide upon confiscation of items impounded.

Article 91

Any violator of provisions of Articles 3, 6, 7, 8, 9, 10, 12, 14, 15, 16 of this law shall be imprisoned for a term not less than one (1) month and not more than three (3) months and/or fined not less than Dh 1000 and not more than Dh 5000. The court may order closing down of the printing press if the owner operates it before he obtains the proper licence provided in Article 3.

Article 92

Any violator of provisions of Articles 25 and 35 of this law, shall be fined not less than Dh 2000 and not more than Dh 5000.

Article 93

For any other violation of provisions of this law the violator shall be fined not less than Dh 1000 and not more than Dh 2000, and/or imprisoned for a term not less than one (1) month and not more than six (6) months.

Article 94

The court may confiscate items seized if the violation is made under Articles 18, 19, 20, 21, 61, 63, 64 and 66 of this law.

Article 95

If the writer, or the graphic designer or the like commits an offence punishable by this law, the editor-in-chief or the editor shall be considered a part of this offence and shall have the same punishment handed to the original violator. Nonetheless, the editor-in-chief or the editor shall be pardoned if he proves that publication is made without his knowledge.

Article 96

If a material, a drawing, a picture, or a symbol, or any similar mean is used to commit an offence punishable by this law and that such material, drawing, picture, symbols or the like are published beyond the UAE boundaries, the importer of the publication or the newspaper in which such materials are published and the circulator shall be a party to this offence unless it is proved that the importer or circulator was unable to know the content of the material.

Article 97

The owner of the newspaper or the publication shall jointly pay along with the editor-in-chief or the editor damages the court orders to be paid to the victim.

Article 98

The press is free within the limits set by the law and it is prohibited to suspend activities or close down newspapers by administrative means unless the press defames Islamic beliefs or incites hatred against the system of ruling, or causes harm to the supreme interests of the country, or publishes materials that cause damage to the constitution, particularly to the concept of unity and federation, or threatens public order, or serves foreign interests that contradict national interests, or if the newspaper is discovered to receive any form of assistance from a foreign country, or publishes ideas of a hostile country, or discloses military secrets, or publishes materials that cause confusion among the public.

The Cabinet, upon a report by the Minister of Information and Culture, shall issue a decision suspending activities of the newspaper for a period not more than one year, or otherwise cancels the licence issued to the newspaper. The Cabinet may also suspend activities of the newspaper for a period not more than one year if it publishes what contradicts the ban provided in Articles 70, 71, 72, 75, and 80. Decision of suspension or cancellation of the licence shall not prejudice the right to bring offenders before the court. In case of extreme need and in circumstances mentioned in the previous paragraph the newspaper may be suspended for a period not more than two weeks and by a ministerial decision provided that the Cabinet is made known of the decision.

Article 99

The common law action for offences punishable by this law extinguishes after three months of the date the offence takes place.

Article 100

A common law action shall not be raised for offences of insult or slander, which take place in newspapers or the like unless by a complaint raised by the complainant to the public prosecution, or a law enforcing official.

If there is more than one complainant, the complaint shall be raised by one of them and if there is more than one defendant and that the complaint is raised against one of them it shall be considered raised against the others.

Article 101

No common law action shall be raised for defamation offence committed by newspapers or other publications against the president of state of an Arab, Islamic or friendly country, or representative of a country to the UAE unless by a request from the minister.

Article 102

No common law action shall be raised for slander or insult offences committed by newspapers other publications against the Federal National Council, army, courts, and other public institutions unless upon a request from the institution or head of the complainant agency.

Article 103

The complainant may disclaim his complaint at any time until a final rule is issued on the common law action. The common law action extinguishes by disclaimer. If there is more than one defendant, the disclaimer shall not be effective unless it is made by all of the complainants.

Disclaimer made for one defendant includes others.

Chapter 9
Miscellaneous

Article 104

Anyone may challenge before courts the final administrative decisions issued by the provisions of this law. The challenge shall be made within sixty (60) days of the date the subject decision is issued.

Article 105

Provisions of this law do not apply to publications issued by ministries, government departments and public institutions issued for the purpose of their activities. Provisions do not apply also to books, publications, and pamphlets issued or imported by the UAE University, or by Ministry of Education for the purpose of using them in its colleges, schools and institutes.

Article 106

Federal law No 5 for 1973 and any other provision that contradicts this law shall be cancelled.

Article 107

The minister shall issue necessary decisions and regulations to implement the law.

Article 108

The law shall be published in the official gazette and shall be effective upon issuance.

Appendix 4: 2010 National Media Council Resolution

Resolution of the Chairman of the Council number (20} of 1431 H/2010 Regarding the Media Content Criterion

Article One

All the visible, audible and legible media means in the country including the free zones areas, shall comply to the criterion of the media contents as stated in the Federal Law number 15 of 1980 regarding the prints and publications and the other prevailing laws and systems

Article Two

Without prejudice to what was stated in the previous article, the Media corporations and means shall comply with the following criterion in particular:

1. Not to abuse the God, Islamic beliefs and to respect all other heaven religions.
2. To respect the regime system in United Arab Emirates and its political symbols and corporations.
3. To respect the cultural and civilization heritage of United Arab Emirates.
4. Not to abuse the national unity and social solidarity and not to ignite the ideological, location and tribal trends
5. To respect the trends and policies adopted by United Arab Emirates at the local level and the level of its relations with other countries.
6. Not to abuse the economical system of the State and not to disseminate misleading and tendentious rumors and news.
7. To respect the state trends to enhance its national identity and merge the nationals in the media business.
8. To respect the moral principles and bonds in the media work
9. Not to disseminate and transmit information that abuses children, women and other categories of the community and that instigate to hatred and violence.
10. To respect the intellectual property rights

Article Three

Each media corporation shall carry out alone the following:

- Assure the respect of the above criterion

1. Top maintain and keep a record and archive that includes all the media materials and preparation that were produced or printed or distributed or transmitted within three consecutive months, and to allow the council to inspect that archive at any time requested.
2. Provide the council with monthly reports on compliance with such criterion.

3. Provide immediate and prompt replies to all matters given by the Council in respect of any remarks or complaints reported by public or any other party.

Article Four

Without prejudice to any other punishments stipulated in the prevailing laws, the council is entitled to take any of the following actions in case of violation:

1. Warning
2. Apology and correction and the right of reply
3. Remove the damage arising from the violation.
4. Suspend the license for the period considered by the Council. 5- Cancel the license.

Article Five

The Department of Following Up the Media Content of the Council shall assure the compliance of the media corporations with the aforesaid criterion.

Article Six

The provisions of this resolution shall be effected from date of issue and to be published in the gazette.

Appendix 5: Cybercrime Law, Sections on Speech

Article 17

Shall be punished by imprisonment and a fine not less than two hundred and fifty thousand dirhams and not in excess of five hundred thousand dirhams or either of these two penalties whoever establishes, manages or runs a website or transmits, sends, publishes or re-publishes through the computer network pornographic materials or gambling activities and whatever that may afflict the public morals.

Shall be punished by the same penalty whoever produces, draws up, prepares, sends or saves for exploitation, distribution, or display to others through the computer network, pornographic materials or gambling activities and whatever that may afflict the public morals.

If the subject of the pornographic content involves a juvenile under eighteen years of age, or if such content is designed to seduce juveniles, the principal shall be punished by imprisonment for a period of at least one year and a fine not less than fifty thousand dirhams and not in excess of one hundred and fifty thousand dirhams.

Article 21

Shall be punished by imprisonment of a period of at least six months and a fine not less than one hundred and fifty thousand dirhams and not in excess of five hundred thousand dirhams or either of these two penalties whoever uses a computer network or and electronic information system or any information technology means for the invasion of privacy of another person in other than the cases allowed by the law and by any of the following ways:

1. Eavesdropping, interception, recording, transferring, transmitting or disclosure of conversations or communications, or audio or visual materials.
2. Photographing others or creating, transferring, disclosing, copying or saving electronic photos.
3. Publishing news, electronic photos or photographs, scenes, comments, statements or information even if true and correct.

Shall also be punished by imprisonment for a period of at least one year and a fine not less than two hundred and fifty thousand dirhams and not in excess of five hundred thousand dirhams or either of these two penalties whoever uses an electronic information system or any information technology means for amending or processing a record, photo or scene for the purpose of defamation of or offending another person or for attacking or invading his privacy.

Article 24

Shall be punished by temporary imprisonment and a fine not less than five hundred thousand dirhams and not in excess of one million dirhams whoever establishes or administer or runs a website or publishes on a computer network or any information technology means which would promote or praise any programs or ideas which would prompt riot, hatred, racism, sectarianism, or damage the national unity or social peace or prejudice the public order and public morals.

Article 2

Shall be punished by temporary imprisonment and a fine not in excess of one million dirhams whoever establishes, manages or runs a website or uses information on the computer network or information technology means with intent to incite acts or publishes or transmits information, news or cartoon drawings or any other pictures which may endanger the national security and the higher interests of the State or afflicts its public order.

Article 29

Shall be punished by temporary imprisonment and a fine not in excess of one million dirhams whoever publishes information, news, statements or rumors on a website or any computer network or information technology means with intent to make sarcasm or damage the reputation, prestige or stature of the State or any of its institutions or its president, vice-president, any of the rulers of the Emirates, their crown princes, or the deputy rulers of the Emirates, the State flag, the national peace, its logo, national anthem or any of its symbols.

Article 30

Shall be punished by life imprisonment whoever establishes, manages or runs a website, or publishes information on the Computer network or information technology means aiming or calling to overthrow, change the ruling system of the State, or seize it or to disrupt the provisions of the constitution or the laws applicable in the country or to oppose the basic principles which constitutes the foundations of the ruling system of the state.

Shall be punished by the same penalty whoever promotes to, incites or facilitates to others the commission of any of the aforementioned acts.

Article 32

Shall be punished by imprisonment and a fine not less than five hundred thousand dirhams and not in excess of one million dirhams or either of these two penalties whoever establishes, manages or runs a website or uses the Computer network or any information technology means for planning, organizing, promoting or calling for demonstrations or protests or the like without license from the competent authority.

Article 38

Shall be punished by temporary imprisonment whoever provides any organizations, institutions, authorities or any other entities through the computer network or any information technology means any incorrect, inaccurate or misleading information which may damage the interests of the State or injures its reputation, prestige or stature.

Article 47

Without prejudice to the provisions of chapter two of part two of book one of the Penal Code, the provisions of this Decree-Law shall apply to any person who has committed any of the crimes mentioned therein outside the country, if its object is an electronic information system, computer network, website or information technology means relates to the federal government or any of the local governments of the Emirates of the State or any authority or public institution owned by any of them.

Appendix 6: UAE Journalists Code of Ethics

1. Respect the truth and the right of the public to have access to the true and accurate information.

2. While performing his duty, the journalist is demanded to commit himself at all times to the principles of freedom and integrity in gathering and publishing stories. He should also voice fair and neutral comments and criticism.

3. A journalist must only publish facts from sources known to him, and must not hide any basic and important information, forge facts of falsify documents.

4. He should use only legitimate means to obtain information, photos and documents from original sources.

5. Publishing news and information of pictures must be examined carefully for accuracy, and their true meaning must not be altered by editing, title or photo comment. All documents must be edited accurately, and any uncertified reports, rumors or speculations must be reported as such. If re-edited or reproduced material was used as a symbolic picture, it should be made clear through the comment that it is not a documentary picture.

6. Journalists undertake to rectify any published information that proved to be wrong and harmful to others.

7. There should be no compromise in credibility.

8. Respecting privacy is a main principle in the profession and journalists should respect the privacy of individuals and not expose it by publishing any thing without the consent of those individuals. If personal conduct over crosses with public interest, such conduct may be covered without violating the personal rights of uninvolved individuals.

9. In regards to the news source, the code and charter stress that professionalism and confidentiality should be strictly observed if the source demands anonymity. The journalist has every right to present evidence or expose their source without the source's consent.

10. Journalists should not seek to provoke or inflame public feelings by any means or use means of excitement and deception or dishonest reporting. They should not use media organs for purpose of libel or slandering.

11. The edited publications should not be influenced by personal interests or businesses with a third party. Publishers and editors-in-chief must turn down any such attempts, and draw a clear line between reported stories and commercial articles or publications.

12. Journalists should be very vigilant to traps of discrimination and avoid involving themselves by any means in any stories hinting to discrimination of race, sex, language, faith or national and social backgrounds.

13. They must be aware that a suspect is innocent until proven guilty, thus names and photos of suspects should not be published until a final verdict is issued.

14. In crimes and issues dealing with children, names and photos should not be published.

15. Journalists must be very careful in their personal relationships with news sources so as these bonds can not impact the Partiality.

16. The media should refrain from publishing photos of brutal violence and respect the feeling of the public especially children.

17. Journalists are urged to avoid using offending and obscene language in their reports.

18. Islam is a basic and important component of UAE culture, values and traditions, and the respect of divine religions and traditions and values of nations takes center stage at the mandatory code of ethics of the media and should not be offended or desecrated by any forms.

19. Human rights should also be respected and valued and should not be abused by the media under any pretext.

20. Plagiarism, ill-intention interpretation, libel, slandering, censure, defamation, allegation and accepting bribery to publish or hide information are all dangerous professional violations.

21. When using facts published by competitors, journalists must give credit to the competitor.

22. Competing for news, pictures and information is a right, provided practicing such competition is honest and clear and does not hinder the work of colleagues in competing publications.

23. A journalist has to do his best not to become part of a story, and to cover news not make them. While gathering information, a journalist may not present himself as anything other than a journalist.

24. Coverage of medical cases must not be sensational, as this can lead to spreading fear or unrealistic hope among readers. Publishing the first stage of results of researches and medical achievements must not be portrayed as final and undisputed.

25. Journalists must not acquire information or pictures through harassment, temptation or violence.

26. Accepting valuable cash and kind gifts may cause a journalist to be biased in his coverage and is considered breach of the code. This does not apply to souvenir gifts given to the public.

Appendices, Appendix 6: UAE Journalists Code of Ethics

Selected Bibliography

Legislation and Case Law

Castells v. Spain (Strasbourgh, France: European Court of Human Rights, April 23, 1992), http://www.elaw.org/node/5580.

Council of Europe: Convention for the Protection of Human Rights and Fundamental Freedoms, 2010, http://conventions.coe.int/treaty/en/Treaties/Html/005.htm.

International Covenant on Civil and Political Rights (Office of the United Nations High Commissioner for Human Rights, 1966), sec. 19, http://www.ohchr.org/EN/ProfessionalInterest/Pages/CCPR.aspx.

Miami Herald Publishing Company v. Tornillo, Oyez, https://www.oyez.org/cases/1973/73-797 (last visited December 9, 2016).

National Media Council, "Resolution of the Chairman Regarding the Media Content Criterion," (Abu Dhabi, UAE: National Media Council, 2010), Appendix 4.

Obbo and Another v. Attorney-General, Uganda, (2004) AHRLR 256 (UgSC 2004), Centre for Human Rights: University of Pretoria, http://www.chr.up.ac.za/index.php/browse-by-subject/486-uganda-obbo-and-another-v-attorney-general-2004-ahrlr-256-ugsc-2004.html.

The Johannesburg Principles on National Security, Freedom of Expression and Access to Information (London: Article 19, 1995), http://www1.umn.edu/humanrts/instree/johannesburg.html#12.TheSupremeCouncil.aspx.

United Arab Emirates Cybercrime Law, Federal Law No. 5 of 2012, Appendix 5.

United Arab Emirates, Constitution, (1971). Appendix 1.

United Arab Emirates, Penal Code, Federal Law, 1987, *see* Appendix 2.

Doctrine

Buckley, Steve, and et al., Broadcasting, Voice, and Accountability: A Public Interest Approach to Policy, Law, and Regulation (World Bank Publications, 2008).

Crook, Tim, Comparative Media Law and Ethics (Routledge, 2010).

Davi, Streckfuss, Truth on Trial in Thailand: Defamation, Treason, and Lèse-majesté (Taylor & Francis, 2011).

Davidson, Christopher M., Abu Dhabi: Oil and Beyond (Columbia University Press, 2009).

Davies, Gillian, Copyright and the Public Interest, 2nd ed. (Sweet & Maxwell, 2002).

Amponsah, Peter, Libel Law, Political Criticism, and Defamation of Public Figures: the United States, Europe, and Australia, Law and Society (New York, N.Y., 2004).

Glasser, Charles, International Libel and Privacy Handbook: A Global Reference for Journalists, Publishers, Webmasters, and Lawyers (John Wiley & Sons, 2010).

Hopkins, W. Wat, ed., Communication and the Law 2012 (Vision Press, 2012).

Kovach, Bill, and Rosenstiel, Tom, The Elements of Journalism: What Newspeople Should Know and The Public Should Expect (Three Rivers Press, 2007).

Milton, John, Aeropagitica: A Speech for the Liberty of Unlicensed Printing to the Parliament of England (Forgotten Books, 2008).

Mullis, Alastair, Carter-Ruck on Libel and Slander, 6th Revised edition (Lexis Nexis UK, 2010).

Pintak, Lawrence, The New Arab Journalist: Mission and Identity in a Time of Turmoil (I. B. Tauris, 2011).

Rugh, William A., Arab Mass Media: Newspapers, Radio, and Television in Arab Politics (Praeger, 2004).

Reports

Abu Dhabi Media Zone Content Creation Guidelines (Abu Dhabi: Media Zone Authority, December 2013), http://www.mzaabudhabi.ae/en/Images/Media%20Zone%20-%20Abu%20Dhabi%20Content%20Code%202016_tcm27-27080.pdf.

Abu Dhabi Media Zone Content Creation Guidelines, (Abu Dhabi, UAE: Abu Dhabi Media Zone, 2011), http://twofour54.com/en/regulatoryaffairs/about-twofour54/mza-licensing.html.

Adams, Simon, and Khoja, Sara, Confidentiality and Your Business in the Middle East (Clyde & Co, July 22, 2010), http://www.mondaq.com/x/106066/employee+rights+labour+relations/Confidentiality+and+your+business+in+the+Middle+East.

Selected Bibliography

African Commission of Human Rights, "Declaration of Principles on Freedom of Expression in Africa," 2002, sec. 12, http://hrlibrary.umn.edu/achpr/expressionfreedomdec.html.

Arab Media Outlook 2011-2015 (Dubai, UAE: Dubai Press Club, 2012), http://www.arabmediaforum.ae/en/amo.aspx.

Article 19, Civil Defamation: Undermining Free Expression (London: Article 19, 2009), http://www.article19.org/resources.php/resource/1427/en/civil-defamation.

BBC Media Profile, "United Arab Emirates" (London: BBC, May 23, 2016), http://www.bbc.co.uk/news/world-middle-east-14704229.

Central Intelligence Agency, "United Arab Emirates," The World Factbook, November 13, 2016, https://www.cia.gov/library/publications/the-world-factbook/geos/ae.html.

El-Nawawy, Mohammed and Strong, Catherine, "Job Satisfaction and Editorial Freedom at Al-Arabiya: Balance While Covering Volatile Middle East News," Arab Media & Society no. 16 (Fall 2012), http://www.arabmediasociety.com/?article=796.

Fitzgerald, Brian, and Olwan, Rami, "Copyright Law in the United Arab Emirates in the Digital Age," European Intellectual Property Review 32, no. 11 (2010): 565–574.

Freedom House, "Freedom of the Press: 2015 Report, United Arab Emirates" (Washington, D.C., 2016), https://freedomhouse.org/report/freedom-press/2015/united-arab-emirates.

Freedom House, Freedom in the World: United Arab Emirates (Washington, D.C.: Freedom House, 2012), http://www.freedomhouse.org/report/freedom-world/2012/united-arab-emirates.

Katzman, Kenneth, The United Arab Emirates (UAE): Issues for U.S. Policy (Washington, D.C.: Congressional Research Service, October 4, 2012).

Kelly, Rebecca, and Procter, Sharon, Defamation and Social Media in the UAE (Dubai, UAE: Clyde & Co, 2012).

Latheef, Faizal. "Legal System and Practice in the United Arab Emirates (Dubai, UAE: Habib al Mulla & Company, 2011), http://www.habibalmulla.com/Mediaresource/45041b47-a820-44a8-8f6f-ebdc47c42d91.pdf.

Lunjevich, Michael, "Comparative Advertising in the UAE," August 4, 2009, http://www.hadefpartners.com/News/pageid/120-137/default.aspx?mediaid=78.

Mansoor, Ahmed, United Arab Emirates: Media Sustainability Index (Washington, D.C.: Irex, 2008).

McCracken, Patti, "Insult Laws: Insulting to Press Freedom" (World Press Freedom Committee, 2010), http://www.freedomhouse.org/sites/default/files/Insult%20Law%20Report.pdf.

McEvers, Kelly, "Outrage Over Torture Video Goes Unheard In UAE : NPR," NPR.org, May 23, 2009, http://www.npr.org/templates/story/story.php?storyId=104498602.

McGinley, Shane, "UAE's Switch to Digital May Spark TV Boom, Says Regulator," Arabian Business, April 26, 2011, http://www.arabianbusiness.com/uae-s-switch-digital-may-spark-tv-boom-says-regulator-396224.html.

Media Legal Defence Initiative, "British Journalist Wins Two Year Criminal Libel Ordeal in Dubai," June 22, 2011, http://www.mediadefence.org/news-story/british-journalist-wins-two-year-criminal-libel-ordeal-dubai.

OpenNet Initiative, "United Arab Emirates," 2009, http://opennet.net/research/profiles/uae.

Patterson, Maggie, and Fullerton, Romayne, "Naming Names: Crime Coverage Rituals in North America, Sweden, and the Netherlands," in Association for Education in Journalism and Mass Communication (St. Louis, MO, 2011), http://citation.allacademic.com/meta/p_mla_apa_research_citation/5/2/0/1/6/p520168_index.html.

Privacy International, "Privacy Issues: Statutory Rules on Privacy, Report: United Arab Emirates (London), accessed December 7, 2012, https://www.privacyinternational.org/reports/united-arab-emirates/ii-privacy-issues.

Reporters Without Borders, "World Report - United Arab Emirates," 2009, http://en.rsf.org/report-united-arab-emirates,150.html.

Reporters Without Borders, 2013 World Press Freedom Index: Dashed Hopes after Spring (Paris, France: Reporters Without Borders), accessed February 6, 2013, http://en.rsf.org/press-freedom-index-2013,1054.html.

Ristow, Bill, "Sword and Shield: Self-Regulation and International Media," (Washington, D.C.: Center for International Media Assistance), accessed January 24, 2013, http://cima.ned.org/publications/research-reports/sword-and-shield-self-regulation-and-international-media.

Siassios, Anita, Regulation of Digital Content in the UAE—Part One (Al Tamimi & Co. Law Firm, June 2012), http://www.tamimi.com/en/publication/publications/section-3/june/regulation-of-digital-content-in-the-uae-part-one.html.

Steyn, Waldo, Advertising Regulations in the UAE (Al Tamimi & Company, September 12, 2012), http://www.tamimi.com/en/publication/publications/section-3/september/advertising-regulations-in-the-uae.html.

Walden, Ruth, Insult Laws: An Insult to Press Freedom (Reston, Va.: World Press Freedom Committee, 2000), http://www.wpfc.org/site/docs/pdf/Insult%20Laws-Text.PDF.

Selected Bibliography

Websites and Online Communications

"A Crippled Fourth Estate," The Qatar Peninsula, accessed December 9, 2016, http://doha.biz/2011/03/05/a-crippled-fourth-estate/.

"About the Ministry," United Arab Emirates Ministry of Culture, Youth and Community Development, accessed January 25, 2013, http://www.mcycd.ae/sites/mcycdvar/en-us/pages/AboutTheMinistry.aspx.

"About TRA," Telecommunications Regulatory Authority (TRA), accessed May 9, 2013, http://www.tra.gov.ae/about_tra.php.

"About UAE," accessed January 25, 2013, http://www.cemc.ae/subindex.aspx?Id=169&Lid=1.

"About Us - Blocking and Unblocking Internet Content," Etisalat, accessed May 10, 2013, http://www.etisalat.ae/eportal/en/corporate/blocking-unblocking.html.

"Blaspheming Facebooker Is 'Unfit'," 7 Days in Dubai, accessed June 23, 2012, http://www.7daysindubai.com/Blaspheming-facebooker-unfit/story-15882708-detail/story.html.

"Call to Blank Out YouTube in Emirates Too," Khaleej Times, March 10, 2009.

"Editorial Policy," Emirates 24/7, para. 8, accessed January 7, 2013, http://www.emirates247.com/editorial-policy-1.153.

"Etisalat Blocks Skype. Du Doesn't. And Neither Blocks Chatroulette. Confusing, Huh?," Kippreport.com, March 18, 2010, http://www.kippreport.com/blog/kipps-blog/etisalat-blocks-skype-du-doesn%e2%80%99t-and-neither-blocks-chatroulette-confusing-huh/.

"Executive Council - Abu Dhabi," The General Secretariat of the Executive Council, accessed May 7, 2013, http://gsec.abudhabi.ae/Sites/GSEC/Navigation/EN/ExecutiveCouncil/picture-gallery.html.

"Five Emiratis Arrested for Threatening UAE Security," The National, April 26, 2011, http://www.thenational.ae/news/uae-news/five-emiratis-arrested-for-threatening-uae-security.

"FNC Discusses Policy of National Media Council on Updating Media Laws," June 5, 2012, http://www.uaeinteract.com/docs/FNC_discusses_policy_of_the_National_Media_Council_on_updating_media_laws/49781.htm.

"International Recognition of Israel," Jewish Virtual Library, accessed May 9, 2013, http://www.jewishvirtuallibrary.org/jsource/Peace/recogIsrael.html.

"Issa Bin Zayed Al Nahyan, Abu Dhabi Royal, Acquitted In Torture Trial (VIDEO)," Huffington Post, January 11, 2010, http://www.huffingtonpost.com/2010/01/11/sheik-issa-bin-zayed-al-n_n_418978.html.

"Licensing of Media Workers," Article 19, accessed March 25, 2013, http://www.article19.org/pages/en/licensing-of-media-workers.html.

"Media Laws And Regulation," National Media Council, accessed May 12, 2013, http://nmc.gov.ae/en/pages/MediaLawsAndRegulation.aspx.

"Prohibited Content Categories," Etisalat, accessed June 23, 2012, http://www.etisalat.ae/assets/document/blockcontent.pdf.

"Radio and Television Channels of Dubai," Wikipedia, the Free Encyclopedia, December 3, 2016, http://en.wikipedia.org/w/index.php?title=Radio_and_television_channels_of_Dubai&oldid=531074366.

"The Supreme Council," The Official Website of the U.A.E. Cabinet, accessed May 7, 2013, http://www.uaecabinet.ae/English/UAEGovernment/Pages/.

"The United Arab Emirates: Getting Twitchy About Democracy," The Economist, June 30, 2011, http://www.economist.com/node/18898137.

"TRA Issues Regulations Policy on 'Internet Access Management'," UAE Interact, February 8, 2008, http://www.uaeinteract.com/docs/TRA_issues_regulation_policy_on_Internet_Access_Management/31367.htm.

"UAE Activist Jailed for Court Tweet," BBC, April 8, 2013, http://www.bbc.co.uk/news/world-middle-east-22071517.

"UAE Newspaper Editors Sign New Code of Ethics," International Journalists Network, November 10, 2007, http://ijnet.org/opportunities/uae-newspaper-editors-sign-new-code-ethics.

https://eng-archive.aawsat.com/theaawsat/media-news/uae-rules-journalists-not-to-be-jailed-over-work.

"UAE Suspends Newspaper over 'Horse Doping' Claims," Arabian Business, accessed December 31, 2012, http://www.arabianbusiness.com/uae-suspends-newspaper-over-horse-doping-claims-16392.html.

"United Arab Emirates Profile," BBC, November 14, 2012, sec. Middle East, para. 12, http://www.bbc.co.uk/news/world-middle-east-14703998.

"United Arab Emirates to Try 94 Accused of Trying to Seize Power," CNN, January 27, 2013, http://www.cnn.com/2013/01/27/world/meast/uae-plot.

"Why Insults Are a Political Issue," The Guardian, May 16, 2012, http://www.guardian.co.uk/law/2012/may/16/why-insults-are-political-issue.

Abdulkhaleq, Abdulla, "Ups and Downs of UAE Rankings," Gulf News, March 6, 2012, para. 12, http://gulfnews.com/opinions/columnists/ups-and-downs-of-uae-rankings-1.990500.

Al Amir, Salam, "Former Deyaar Chief Zack Shahin Back in UAE Custody," September 2, 2012, http://www.thenational.ae/news/uae-news/former-deyaar-chief-zack-shahin-back-in-uae-custody.

Al Gergawi, Mishaal, "Incommunicado: The State of the Gulf," Gulf News, April 17, 2011, para. 11, http://gulfnews.com/opinions/columnists/incommunicado-the-state-of-the-gulf-1.794063#.UO7euwvQJQQ.twitter.

Selected Bibliography

Al Theeb, Allia, "Draft Media Law: Journalists 'Will Insist on Changes'," Gulf News, April 28, 2009, http://gulfnews.com/news/gulf/uae/media/draft-media-law-journalists-will-insist-on-changes-1.65700.

Al-Qassemi, Sultan, "Pioneer Bloggers in the Gulf Arab States," Jadaliyya, December 20, 2012, para. 10, http://www.jadaliyya.com/pages/index/3643/pioneer-bloggers-in-the-gulf-arab-states.

Amir, Al, "Dubai Police Chief Defamed on Twitter, Court Hears," February 29, 2012, http://www.thenational.ae/news/uae-news/courts/dubai-police-chief-defamed-on-twitter-court-hears.

Amnesty International, End "travesty of Justice" for Five Convicted over President Insults, Nov. 21, 2011, https://www.amnesty.org/en/latest/news/2011/11/uae-end-travesty-justice-five-convicted-over-insults/.

Barrett, Liz," New Editor-in-Chief 'Appointed' For Abu Dhabi's National," Columbia Journalism Review, accessed January 21, 2013, http://www.cjr.org/the_kicker/new_editorinchief_appointed_fo.php.

Brass, Kevin, Personal Communication, Email, April 30, 2013.

Casciani, Dominic, "Prosecutors Clarify Offensive Online Posts Law," BBC, December 19, 2012, sec. UK, http://www.bbc.co.uk/news/uk-20777002.

Committee to Protect Journalists, "CPJ Concerned About UAE Draft Media Law," March 9, 2009, http://cpj.org/2009/03/cpj-concerned-about-uae-draft-media-law.php.

Davidson, Christopher, "The Making of a Police State," Foreign Policy, April 14, 2011, http://www.foreignpolicy.com/articles/2011/04/14/the_making_of_a_police_state.

Duffy, Matt, "'Cultures of Journalism' in Arabic- and English-language Newspapers Within the United Arab Emirates," Journal of Middle East Media 9, no. 1 (2013).

Duffy, Matt, "Challenges Facing Press Freedom," Gulf News, February 10, 2012, http://gulfnews.com/opinions/columnists/challenges-facing-press-freedom-1.978338.

Duffy, Matt, "Civil Courts Should Handle Defamation," Gulf News, November 18, 2011, http://gulfnews.com/opinions/columnists/civil-courts-should-handle-defamation-1.932729.

Duffy, Matt, "Journalists Should Never Compromise on Integrity," Gulf News, March 9, 2012, http://gulfnews.com/opinions/columnists/journalists-should-never-compromise-on-integrity-1.991869.

Duffy, Matt, "Newspapers Inconsistent over Activist Arrests," Mideastposts.com, April 12, 2011, http://mideastposts.com/2011/04/12/uae-press-inconsistent-over-handling-of-blogger-arrests/.

Duffy, Matt, "Obstacles to Liberty," Index on Censorship 41, no. 4 (December 1, 2012): 48–54.

Duffy, Matt, "Peninsula Journalism Attack Resonates Regionally," Mideast Posts, June 6, 2011, http://mideastposts.com/2011/03/peninsula-attack-on-journalism-rings-true-region-wide/.

Duffy, Matt, "Revised Media Law for the UAE," Gulf News, accessed January 11, 2013, http://gulfnews.com/opinion/thinkers/revised-media-law-for-the-uae-1.998464.

Duffy, Matt, "UAE Arrests Activist For 'False News' Tweets," Al Monitor, March 27, 2013, http://www.al-monitor.com/pulse/originals/2013/03/twitter-arrest-uae-social-media-law-trial.html.

Duffy, Matt., "CNN Asks UAE Leader About Freedom of Speech, Press," blog, December 6, 2011, para. 4, http://mattjduffy.com/2011/12/cnn-free-speech-interview, para. 5.

Editor, "The National, the UAE's New Quality English Newspaper, Launches in Abu Dhabi," Media Middle East, April 20, 2008, para. 4, Retrieved September 16, 2011, from http://mediame.com/news/announcement/the_national_the_uaes_new_quality_english_newspaper_launches_in_abu_dhabi.

El-Baltaji, Dana, "Emirates Press Law," Arab Media & Society, Fall 2009, http://www.arabmediasociety.com/?article=727.

Fenton, Jenifer, "Crackdown on Islamists in the UAE," The Arabist, August 4, 2012, http://arabist.net/blog/2012/8/4/crackdown-on-islamists-in-the-uae.html.

Greenslade, Roy, "UAE Aims to Stifle Press Freedom," The Guardian, April 16, 2009, http://www.guardian.co.uk/media/greenslade/2009/apr/16/dubai-press-freedom.

Habboush, Mahmoud. "UAE Nationals Ask: Why Can't We All Vote?," Huffington Post, September 21, 2011, http://www.huffingtonpost.com/2011/09/21/uae-nationals-ask-why-ca_n_973656.html.

Hamid, Triska, "National Media Council Tells Advertisers to Keep Their Lingo Local," The National, January 17, 2013, http://www.thenational.ae/thenationalconversation/industry-insights/media/national-media-council-tells-advertisers-to-keep-their-lingo-local.

Hammond, Andrew, "UAE Media Fear Fines, Jail in New Draft Law," Reuters, April 9, 2009, http://www.reuters.com/article/2009/04/13/emirates-media-law-idUSLD4731820090413;

Hooglund, Eric and Toth, Anthony, A Country Study: United Arab Emirates (Washington, D.C.: Library of Congress, 2007), http://lcweb2.loc.gov/frd/cs/aetoc.html.

Howard, Philip, "The Arab Spring's Cascading Effects," Miller-McCune, February 23, 2011, https://psmag.com/economics/the-cascading-effects-of-the-arab-spring-28575.

Human Rights Watch, "Just the Good News, Please," April 6, 2009, http://www.hrw.org/news/2009/04/06/just-good-news-please.

Selected Bibliography

Human Rights Watch, "UAE: Civil Society Crackdown Widens," May 3, 2011, http://www.hrw.org/news/2011/05/03/uae-civil-society-crackdown-widens.

Human Rights Watch, "UAE: Cybercrimes Decree Attacks Free Speech," November 28, 2012, http://www.hrw.org/news/2012/11/28/uae-cybercrimes-decree-attacks-free-speech.

Human Rights Watch, "UAE: Media Law Undermines Free Expression," April 13, 2009, http://www.hrw.org/news/2009/04/13/uae-media-law-undermines-free-expression.

IREX, "Oman Media Sustainability Index (Washington, D.C.: IREX, 2009), http://www.irex.org/resource/oman-media-sustainability-index-msi.

Khalifa,, Reem, "Saudis, Other Gulf Nations Send Force to Bahrain," The (U.K.) Guardian, March 14, 2011, http://www.guardian.co.uk/world/feedarticle/9545419.

Mills, Andrew, "A Vision in the Desert," Columbia Journalism Review, May 22, 2009, http://www.cjr.org/feature/a_vision_in_the_desert.php.

Morris, Loveday, "Arabic Daily Suspended over Horse-doping Libel," The National, July 3, 2009, para. 2, http://www.thenational.ae/news/uae-news/arabic-daily-suspended-over-horse-doping-libel.

National Staff, "FNC shocked by 'baseless' European human rights report," October 29, 2012, http://www.thenational.ae/news/uae-news/fnc-shocked-by-baseless-european-human-rights-report.

Peel, Michael, Hall, Camilla Hall and Allam, Abeer, "UAE Cracks down on Internet Dissent," Financial Times, November 13, 2012, http://www.ft.com/intl/cms/s/0/243afa46-2da9-11e2-9988-00144feabdc0.html#axzz2Id9h7YNH.

Potter, Sam, "Financial Crisis in the UAE - A Paralysis of Analysis," Arab Media & Society, Spring 2010, 2, http://www.arabmediasociety.com/topics/index.php?t_article=286.

Rasheed, Abdulla, "Freedom and Responsibility Go Together to Secure State's Interest," Gulf News (Dubai, February 22, 2011), para. 3, http://gulfnews.com/news/gulf/uae/media/freedom-and-responsibility-go-together-to-secure-state-s-interest-1.765596.

Rasheed, Abdullah, "Emarat Al Youm Suspended as of Today," Gulf News, July 5, 2009, http://gulfnews.com/news/gulf/uae/media/emarat-al-youm-suspended-as-of-today-1.500173.

Rasheed, Abdullah, "The Ceiling of Press Freedom in UAE Is Falling," Gulf News, March 2, 2010, http://gulfnews.com/opinions/columnists/the-ceiling-of-press-freedom-in-uae-is-falling-1.590497.

Reporters Without Borders, "Authorities Bend Rules to Block Access to Online Magazine," July 2, 2010, http://en.rsf.org/united-arab-emirates-court-closes-independent-website-14-01-2010,36104.html.

Reporters without Borders, "Authorities Crack down on Social Networks and Activist Bloggers," para. 3., https://rsf.org/en/news/authorities-crack-down-social-networks-and-activist-bloggers.

Reporters Without Borders, "Court Closes Libel Case Against Website Reporter," December 3, 2007, http://en.rsf.org/united-arab-emirates-court-closes-libel-case-against-03-12-2007,24444.html.

Reporters Without Borders, "Newspaper Suspended for 20 Days over Story Race Horse," July 7, 2009, http://en.rsf.org/united-arab-emirates-newspaper-suspended-for-20-days-07-07-2009,33730.html.

Rizvi, Raza, Personal communication, email, March 31, 2013.

Sabah, Zaid, "Islamists in U.A.E Had Links With 'External Elements': WAM," Bloomberg, August 12, 2012, http://www.bloomberg.com/news/2012-08-13/islamists-in-u-a-e-had-links-with-external-elements-wam.html.

Salama, Samir, and Al Jandaly, Bassma, "Shaikh Khalifa to Open New FNC Term," Gulf News, November 15, 2011, http://gulfnews.com/news/gulf/uae/government/shaikh-khalifa-to-open-new-fnc-term-1.930855.

Salem, Ola, "Islah 'Does Not Represent UAE Interests'," The National, accessed May 9, 2013, http://www.thenational.ae/news/uae-news/islah-does-not-represent-uae-interests.

Sambridge, Andy, "Action Plan Call to Secure UAE's National Identity," Arabian Business, August 11, 2011, http://www.arabianbusiness.com/action-plan-call-secure-uae-s-national-identity-415890.html.

Samir, Samir, "UAE Upholds Press Freedom," Gulf News, September 25, 2007, http://gulfnews.com/news/gulf/uae/media/uae-upholds-press-freedom-1.202309.

Sengupta, Chiranjib, "Decoding the Cultural Divide in the UAE," Gulf News, June 2, 2012, http://gulfnews.com/news/gulf/uae/society/decoding-the-cultural-divide-in-the-uae-1.1030647.

Shah, Angela, "United Arab Emirates Step Up Efforts to Counter Dissent," The New York Times, May 30, 2012, http://www.nytimes.com/2012/03/22/world/middleeast/22iht-m22-uae-islamists.html.

Sharma, Rahul, "Journalists Have Nothing to Fear: Director General, National Media Council," Khaleej Times, February 9, 2009, http://www.khaleejtimes.com/DisplayArticleNew.asp?col=&section=theuae&xfile=data/theuae/2009/February/theuae_February188.xml.

Spencer, Richard, "Naval Battle Between UAE and Saudi Arabia Raises Fears for Gulf Security," The Telegraph, March 26, 2010, sec. worldnews, http://www.telegraph.co.uk/news/worldnews/middleeast/unitedarabemirates/7521219/Naval-battle-between-UAE-and-Saudi-Arabia-raises-fears-for-Gulf-security.html.

Staff, "Expats Make up over 88% of UAE Population," Emirates 24/7, April 17, 2011, http://www.emirates247.com/news/expats-make-up-over-88-of-uae-population-2011-04-17-1.381853.

Selected Bibliography

Surk, Barbara, "5 UAE Convicted Reform Activists Freed from Jail," Boston.com, November 28, 2011, http://www.boston.com/news/world/middleeast/articles/2011/11/28/uae_president_pardons_5_convicted_activists/.

The Arabic Network for Human Rights Information, "In Support of Freedom of Expression ANHRI Calls the UAE Judiciary to a Different Legal Approach to Handle the Case of Chief Editor of "Hetta" E-magazine," October 10, 2009, http://www.anhri.net/en/reports/2009/pr1010.shtml.

Von Riedemann, Dominic, "UAE Blocks Ahmed and Salim Cartoon," Suite 101, March 4, 2009, http://suite101.com/article/uae-blocks-ahmed-and-salim-cartoon-a100275.

Walter, Vic, et al., "Torture Tape Implicates UAE Royal Sheikh," ABC News, April 22, 2009, http://abcnews.go.com/Blotter/story?id=7402099.

WAM, "Journalists and Writers Associations Slam HRW Report" (Abu Dhabi, UAE: Emirates News Agency (WAM), January 27, 2011), http://www.uaeinteract.com/docs/Journalists_and_writers_associations_slam_HRW_report_/44235.htm.

WAM, "National Media Council Gets Consultative Panel," Gulf News, March 21, 2013, http://m.gulfnews.com/news/uae/national-media-council-gets-consultative-panel-1.1161288.

WAM, "National Media Council Issues Advertising Content Regulation," Breitbart.com, January 16, 2013, para. 1, http://www.breitbart.com/system/wire/upi20130116-123010-2998.

WAM, "UAE National Media Council Welcomes All Debates on Draft Media Law," Gulf News, April 13, 2009, para. 8, http://gulfnews.com/news/gulf/uae/media/uae-national-media-council-welcomes-all-debates-on-draft-media-law-1.63826.

Wigglesworth, Robin, "Rights Group Attacks UAE Draft Media Law," Financial Times, April 13, 2009, http://www.ft.com/cms/s/0/58ccf69c-2817-11de-8dbf-00144feabdc0.html#axzz2SuInXicX.

Za'Za, Bassam, "Broadcaster Fined Dh10,000 for Defaming Preacher," Gulf News, May 25, 2011, http://gulfnews.com/news/gulf/uae/crime/broadcaster-fined-dh10-000-for-defaming-preacher-1.812541.

Selected Bibliography

Index

The numbers here refer to paragraph numbers.